HOLLYWOOD HEAVEN

From Valentino to John Belushi
the film stars who died young

DAVID BARRACLOUGH

GALLERY BOOKS
An imprint of W.H. Smith Publishers Inc.
112 Madison Avenue
New York, New York 10016

*To my Folks, for many things,
but especially all the taping.*

A QUINTET BOOK

Produced for
GALLERY BOOKS
an imprint of W. H. Smith Publishers, Inc.
112 Madison Avenue
New York, New York 10016

ISBN 0-8317-4528-2

This book was designed and produced by
Quintet Publishing Limited
6 Blundell Street
London N7 9BH

Creative Director: Terry Jeavons
Designer: Stuart Walden
Artworker: Jenny Millington
Project Editor: Judith Simons

Typeset in Great Britain by
Central Southern Typesetters, Eastbourne
Manufactured in Hong Kong by
Regent Publishing Services Limited
Printed in Hong Kong by
Leefung-Asco Printers Limited

ACKNOWLEDGEMENTS

Special thanks to Jane Millichip for her invaluable
help and advice during the preparation of the
manuscript, to my editor, Judith Simons, and to Frank
Sidebottom, Ian Dury and Wreckless Eric for
providing a constant source of inspiration.

CREDITS

Key: t = top; b = bottom; l = left; r = right;
c = centre.

The publishers would like to extend special thanks to
the **Joel Finler Collection** for providing the majority
of the pictures featured in this book. They would also
like to thank the following:

Aquarius Literary Agency and Picture Library:
pages 14, 16 r, 19, 29, 40 b, 42, 44 tr, 47 t, 49 l r,
52 l r, 54 l, 55, 65 l, 66 t, 67 t, 68 b, 76 t bl, 82 t,
84 l, 85 t, 88 l, 89 l. **David Barraclough:** pages
26 tr, 40 tr, 47 b, 63, 65 r, 69 b, 76 br, 91 t. **Joel
Finler Collection:** all images not otherwise credited.
John Frost Historical Newspaper Service: pages
8 b, 9 tr b, 10 tr br, 11 b, 24 b, 34 b, 44 tl, 54 b,
56 b, 69 c, 71 tl b, 73 bl, 75 b, 86 b.

The Publishers would also like to acknowledge the
following film companies involved in the distribution
and/or production of the films illustrated in the book,
and apologize for any unintentional omissions:

American International Pictures: *Die Monster Die,
Dillinger, Sergeant Deadhead.* **Columbia:** *The Big
Heat, From Here to Eternity, It Happened One Night,
Ship of Fools, Twentieth Century.* **Walt Disney
Productions:** *Treasure Island.* **Enterprise:** *Body
and Soul.* **Douglas Fairbanks:** *The Gaucho.* **Charles
K Feldman/Elia Kazan:** *A Streetcar Named Desire.*
Howard Hughes: *Hell's Angels.* **IFD:** *The African
Queen.* **Lippert:** *Superman and the Mole Men.*
London Films: *Anna Karenina, Fire Over England.*
Metro: *The Four Horsemen of the Apocalypse.* **MGM:**
*The Big Parade, The Blackboard Jungle, Brainstorm,
Camille, China Seas, The Clock, The Crowd, Executive
Suite, The Fastest Guitar Alive, The Fearless Vampire
Killers, The Flesh and the Devil, Gone With the Wind,
Jailhouse Rock, Meet Me in St Louis, The Pirate, The
Postman Always Rings Twice, Queen Christina, Red
Dust, Test Pilot, That Midnight Kiss, Till the Clouds
Roll By, Viva Las Vegas, The Wizard of Oz.* **Papillon
Partnership:** *Papillon.* **Paramount:** *The Affairs of
Anatol, Horse Feathers, Shane, This Gun For Hire.*
Gabriel Pascal: *Pygmalion.* **RKO:** *Citizen Kane,
Clash by Night, Of Human Bondage, They Knew What
They Wanted.* **Hal Roach:** *One Million BC.* **Solar:** *Le
Mans, Nevada Smith.* **SNC:** *A Bout de Souffle.*
Twentieth Century Fox: *The Big Lift, Blood and
Sand, Bus Stop, Fixed Bayonets, The Lodger, Miracle
on 34th Street, Niagara, Return of the Jedi, River of No
Return, The Sand Pebbles, The Seven Year Itch, The
Undefeated, Will Success Spoil Rock Hunter?* **United
Artists:** *Baby Face Nelson, The Eagle, Exodus, The
Great Escape, I Want to Live, Judgment at Nuremberg,
The Misfits, Pressure Point, Red River, Son of the
Sheik, Valdez is Coming, West Side Story.* **Universal:**
*Abbott and Costello Meet Frankenstein, Arabian
Nights, The Blues Brothers, The Dark Crystal,
Frankenstein.* **Universal-International:** *All That
Heaven Allows, Ride Clear of Diablo.* **Warwick:** *The
Black Knight.* **Warner Brothers:** *The Big Sleep,
Captain Blood, Dive Bomber, Dodge City, East of
Eden, Gold Diggers of 1933, It's a Great Feeling, The
Maltese Falcon, The Mask of Dimitrios, The Petrified
Forest, The Public Enemy, Rebel Without a Cause, The
Return of Dr X, Rio Bravo, The Sea Hawk, Splendor in
the Grass, Strangers on a Train, Whatever Happened to
Baby Jane?, White Heat.*

MAIN CONTENTS

SPECIAL FEATURES

FOREWORD

The selection of stars for *Hollywood Heaven* proved a difficult task, despite there being a number of essential entries such as Dean, Clift, Valentino, Monroe and Bogart. After some deliberation, I decided not to include anyone who died over the age of 60 nor anyone who made their name outside Hollywood; thus no Richard Burton, Peter Sellers or Bruce Lee. It also meant excluding personal favourites Laurence Harvey, Michael Reeves and Graham Moffatt. Most were also either still acting or at least in the public eye at the time of their deaths, although there are some exceptions, such as the failed child stars.

Nevertheless, readers will no doubt still find some of their favourites missing. I regret there was no room for Roy William Neill (1890–1946), the underrated director of Universal's Sherlock Holmes series, and *Forever Amber* star Linda Darnell (1921–1965). But my aim was to cover the breadth of Hollywood, to include some lesser-known characters at the expense of a few more famous names, and in any case some omissions are inevitable in a 96-page book.

Finally, a word about dates and film titles. A film's year of release does differ from book to book and, in general, I have included the most commonly used date. Similarly, film titles will differ from country to country. In this case I have given the film's original title first, followed by its alternative American or British title in brackets.

■ ■ ■
RIGHT
Valentino, with Vilma Banky, in his last film, *Son of the Sheik* (1926). They had starred together in *The Eagle* the previous year.
■ ■ ■

RUDOLPH VALENTINO

Rudolph Valentino was *the* male sex symbol of the silent era, rivalled only by Douglas Fairbanks. Such was his popularity that his death from peritonitis provoked a number of suicides and over 100,000 fans visited the New York funeral parlour where his half-open casket lay. However, today, more people have probably seen Ken Russell's rather fanciful 1977 biopic than one of Valentino's films.

Valentino was born Rodolfo Alfonzo Raffaelo Pierre Filibert Guglielmi di Valentina d'Antoguolla on 6 May 1895 in Castellaneta, southern Italy. He arrived in America in late 1913 and made his movie debut the next year, probably as an extra in *My Official Wife* (1914), although no copy of the film survives. A number of nondescript roles followed, with Valentino often cast as a villain. It was not until *The Four Horsemen of the Apocalypse* (1921) that his image as 'The World's Greatest Lover' truly emerged and was embraced by millions of women.

Much of his success he owed to MGM script-writer June Mathis, who had been impressed by his performance in *The Wonderful Chance* (1920) and scripted not only *The Four Horsemen* but also a number of his other films over the next few years. The hits now began to flow: *Camille* (1921), *The Sheik* (1921) – perhaps the archetypal Valentino vehicle, a wildly romantic melodrama – and *Blood and Sand* (1922) appeared over the next two years. His popularity was sustained throughout the final years of the silent era with some impressive films. *Monsieur Beaucaire* was a hit in 1924 (and later remade as a vehicle for Bob Hope!), while in 1925 he teamed up with stylish director Clarence Brown to make the elegant film *The Eagle* (1925). His last film, in 1926, was another big hit, *Son of the Sheik*.

RUDOLPH VALENTINO in "THE EAGLE"

Famed gossip columnist Louella Parsons called this movie 'The very picture for which the world's wife, mother and daughter have been waiting!' This was the last great year of the silent movies, as the success of *The Jazz Singer* (1927) the following year heralded the talking picture. It is hard to see how Valentino, with his extravagant acting style even by silent standards, would have survived the coming of the talkies.

■ ■ ■
ABOVE
The Eagle (1925) is Valentino's finest film.
■ ■ ■

■ ■ ■
LEFT
Valentino (right) with director Rex Ingram on the set of *The Four Horsemen of the Apocalypse* (1921).
■ ■ ■

Valentino's private life is perhaps better remembered now than his films. Both his marriages were unsuccessful. In 1919 he married Jean Acker, a union which was never consummated and quickly resulted in divorce. He then married Natacha Rambova (her real name was the rather more mundane Winifred Hudnut), a protégée of lesbian actress Alla Nazimova, before his divorce from Acker was legal. Rambova, who had been the set designer on *Camille*, had great artistic pretensions and was to exert strict control over his career. This relationship not only led to wranglings with Paramount, but also fuelled rumours that Valentino was homosexual and the plaything of two lesbians. There were also personal attacks from the newspapers, one of which labelled Valentino and his followers 'pink powder puffs' and questioned his virility. Such articles were undoubtedly prompted, at least in part, by jealousy; Valentino was a foreigner and, unlike Fairbanks, not an ideal all-American men would aspire to. These details today tend to overshadow his films, which, in at least the case of *The Eagle*, is unfortunate.

'They had so much trouble on their picture (Cobra, 1925) that they had to send for June Mathis, who had written the script for The Four Horsemen of The Apocalypse. The reason was that Natacha, his wife, was writing the script. Every night she would go into a trance and the spirits would come to do spirit writing, and she would write the script. This is what June told me. And in the morning, there would be this great roll of stuff they couldn't shoot because it was quite illegible.' – Silent star Colleen Moore in Hollywood: The Pioneers, by Kevin Brownlow.

ASKS WARRANTS IN BAR FIXING
HOME EDITION
WISCONSIN NEWS
The Peach
TWO CENTS   MILWAUKEE, MONDAY, AUGUST 23, 1926
VALENTINO IS DEAD!
DIES BRAVELY
Sheik Dies Nonchalantly Asking for More Sunlight

SCANDAL

During the early 1920s a series of scandals rocked Hollywood, resulting in a strong public outcry against its hedonistic lifestyle and in a self-imposed and exceedingly strict censorship code that survived almost intact until the mid 1960s. The most famous of these cases was the trial of Roscoe 'Fatty' Arbuckle (1887–1933) after the death of 25-year-old starlet Virginia Rappe. Rappe had been taken ill at a party thrown by the popular comedian on 5 September 1921 and died four days later. It was rumoured that Arbuckle had sexually assaulted Rappe and he was tried on three occasions for involuntary manslaughter.

The first two trials ended with the juries unable to reach an agreement, but at the third attempt Arbuckle was pronounced innocent and the State heavily criticized for charging him in the first place. However, the damage was done, not least through the savage treatment he received from the press. Public feeling was so strong that, during the trial, his wife was shot at outside the court. Hollywood abandoned him, the studios preventing his friends from testifying on his behalf through fear that their stars might become associated with the scandal. Arbuckle's career was effectively over, his reputation permanently tarnished. The studios quickly dropped him and he resorted to working under a pseudonym, William Goodrich, after Buster Keaton had suggested the name 'Will B Good'. He died a broken man, from angina pectoris, in New York on 29 June 1933, aged 46.

There then followed, in rapid succession, the deaths of director William Desmond Taylor and leading actor Wallace Reid. The death of former British army officer Taylor (1877–1922) on the night of 1 February 1922 is one of Hollywood's great

▪ ▪ ▪

BOTTOM LEFT
Actress Virginia Rappe, who died at a party thrown by Arbuckle.

▪ ▪ ▪

BOTTOM RIGHT
During the 1910s, Arbuckle was earning $7,000 per week.

▪ ▪ ▪

BELOW
Fatty Arbuckle, standing with his relatives and members of the jury, at the end of his third trial.

▪ ▪ ▪

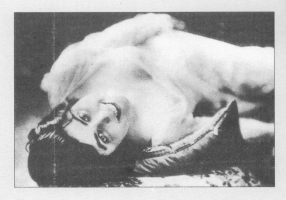

unsolved murders. He was shot in the study of his bungalow. The scandal that followed suggested that Taylor, thought at one time to be homosexual, was pursuing relationships with top stars Mabel Normand and Mary Miles Minter, as well as Minter's mother. Both Minter and Normand had visited Taylor on the night of the murder. There was also an unidentified third visitor, someone who was dressed like a man but who, according to one of Taylor's neighbours, walked like a woman. This led to the theory that the murderer may have been Mary Minter's mother in drag. To add fuel to the scandal, the press also uncovered a 'dope angle' to the case. Not surprisingly, all this publicity had a disastrous effect on the careers of Minter and Normand, ending both.

The following year it was the turn of Wallace Reid (1891–1923), then one of Hollywood's biggest stars. The unfortunate Reid developed an addiction to morphine while filming *Valley of the Giants* (1919). When Reid hurt his leg just before filming was completed at the Oregon locations, the studio sent its doctor to treat him with morphine shots in order to prevent costly delays. Unfortunately, the

10

doctor was rather too efficient in his job and Reid became addicted. Furthermore, Reid was such an important star that Paramount was unwilling to allow him the time for a proper recovery. It was not until March 1922 that he was finally admitted to a sanatorium. He suffered a painful death on 18 January 1923. Reid was only 32.

This was the era of Prohibition and the public outcry against these and other scandals, partly generated by a press eager to boost its circulation figures, was loud and strong. Hollywood was undeniably worried. In particular it feared outside interference. Its response was to install the Postmaster General, Will H Hays, as spokesman for the industry in the position of President of the Motion Picture Producers and Distributors Association of America (MPPDAA, popularly known as The Hays Office). His first significant act was to insist on a morality clause being written into every star's contract, enabling the studios to drop anyone who became tainted by scandal. This was followed in 1927 by a set of guidelines for producers, although it was mostly ignored until another wave of anti-Hollywood publicity in the early 1930s caused the studios to reconsider. This time the Hays Code was rigidly adopted by all the major film producers and held sway for the next 30 years.

'Acquittal is not enough for Roscoe Arbuckle. We feel that a great injustice has been done him . . . There was not the slightest proof adduced to connect him in any way with the commission of a crime. He was manly throughout the case and told a straightforward story which we all believed. We wish him great success and hope that the American people will take the judgement of 14 men and women that Roscoe Arbuckle is entirely innocent and free from all blame.' – Statement from the foreman of the jurors on the Arbuckle case.

Peg Entwistle (1908–1932)

In 1932 British-born Peg Entwistle was just one of thousands of starlets struggling for a break in Hollywood. That year she landed a role in the mystery thriller Thirteen Women *(1932), starring Ricardo Cortez and Irene Dunne. But no more parts came her way. She finally secured her 15 minutes of fame by jumping from the 'Hollywoodland' sign, having climbed to the top of the 50-foot (15-metre) letter 'H'.*

■ ■ ■
ABOVE
The famous 'Hollywoodland' sign, from which Peg Entwistle committed suicide.
■ ■ ■

■ ■ ■
LEFT
The murder of William Desmond Taylor made front page headlines, and reports continued to appear as the mystery surrounding his death deepened.
■ ■ ■

TAYLOR MURDER SUSPECT TRACED TO, FROM HOUSE.

Asked Oil Station Man the Way to Slain Director's Home; Seen Leaving, Boarding Car.

1895 ★ 1936

JOHN GILBERT

John Gilbert is sound cinema's most famous victim. The myth still prevails that he had an unusually high-pitched voice, making it unsuitable for talkies and ending his career. This is patently wrong, as a viewing of his best known talkie, *Queen Christina* (1933), will testify.

Gilbert, who came from a theatrical family, made his movie debut in 1915 and spent the next ten years in routine roles. But in 1924 his luck changed when he signed to MGM and the following year he was offered a role in Erich Von Stroheim's *The Merry Widow* (1925), initially against Von Stroheim's wishes. This was followed by the lead in King Vidor's anti-war classic *The Big Parade* (1925), not only one of Hollywood's finest silent films but also one of the biggest money-makers of the 1920s. It was his fine performance in *The Big Parade* which sealed his star status, although both pictures were to be named on the *New York Times* prestigious ten best films of the year list. However, the films for which Gilbert is best remembered are the generally inferior movies he made with Greta Garbo, starting with the successful *The Flesh and the Devil* (1926) directed by Clarence Brown. This was then followed by *Love* (1927), Garbo's first portrayal of Anna Karenina for which the

distributors provided an alternative happy ending for those exhibitors who desired it, and *A Woman of Affairs* (1928).

It is not so much the films that are well remembered as Gilbert's partnership, and off-screen relationship, with Garbo. Some accounts suggest the love affair started as a publicity stunt while others, including Clarence Brown, insists it began during the first scene they shot on *The Flesh and the Devil*. Whichever is true they were undoubtedly in love, Gilbert soon proposed to Garbo, and the wedding was planned. However, Garbo failed to appear and Gilbert became involved in a violent argument with the powerful Louis B Mayer, which resulted in a permanent rift. Mayer was head of production at MGM, where Gilbert was under contract.

Nevertheless, the Gilbert-Garbo myth is so strong that their ill-fated relationship has totally eclipsed Gilbert's four marriages to actresses Olivia Burwell, Leatrice Joy, Ina Claire (whom Gilbert married on the rebound from Garbo) and Virginia Bruce in the public's memory.

Yet worse was to come for Gilbert. Everyone in Hollywood was in a state of panic over the introduction of talking pictures and each major star's first talkie was awaited with some trepidation. Gilbert's first was *His Glorious Night* (1929; *Breath of Scandal*). He had to deal with some awful dialogue which, combined with his silent acting style, provoked laughter from the audience and poor reviews from the critics. It also probably provided the inspiration for *Singin' in the Rain* (1952). Rumours have surfaced that the film was deliberately sabotaged by Louis B Mayer who ordered the sound engineers to alter Gilbert's voice, although this is unlikely.

■ ■ ■

BELOW
Gilbert was a rapidly fading star by the time he made his final film with Garbo, *Queen Christina* (1933). Nevertheless, this scene at the inn is justly famous, as Garbo memorizes the room by touching all the objects, and the film was a commercial success.

■ ■ ■

Gilbert began to drink heavily. By 1933 his career was on the skids when Garbo offered him the lead in *Queen Christina* after turning down Leslie Howard and sacking Laurence Olivier. The teaming worked well and the film was a hit, but it failed to rescue Gilbert's career. His last film came the following year with the Lewis Milestone comedy

The Captain Hates the Sea (1934). At this time Gilbert was living with Marlene Dietrich, who secured him the lead in her latest picture, *Desire* (1936). However, his heavy drinking persisted and he had a heart attack, losing the role in the process. He died from another heart attack, just as *Desire* went into production. But that was not quite the end of the story. Gilbert's rapid decline, which coincided with his wife Ina Claire's increasing success, partly provided the inspiration for *A Star is Born*. The first version, starring Frederic March and Janet Gaynor, was released a year after his death.

The Captain Hates the Sea *featured a cast of noted drinkers, particularly Gilbert and Victor McLaglen, with the result that production slipped further and further over budget and behind schedule at its Catalina Island locations. The studio, Columbia, began to worry and sent a cable saying, 'Return at once. The cost is staggering', to which they received the reply, 'So is the cast'.*

JEAN HARLOW

Jean Harlow, the Platinum Blonde, became a star after slipping into something a little more comfortable in Howard Hughes's early sound epic, *Hell's Angels* (1930), having made her film debut only two years earlier. During her short career she seemed to personify sex on the screen, not surprisingly encountering a number of problems with the censors.

Harlow's first two years in Hollywood consisted of a few unimportant roles, including a number of Laurel and Hardy shorts, before *Hell's Angels* dramatically launched her career. The film was already completed, with Greta Nissen in the Harlow role, when sound became essential to a film's success. Hughes wanted to reshoot, but Nissen's accent made her unsuitable for the role. Fortunately for Harlow, she shared the same agent

...
BELOW
Hell's Angels (1930) is the movie that made Jean Harlow a star. She is seen here on intimate terms with the film's hero, Ben Lyon.
...

as Nissen, who convinced Hughes that she would be perfect for the part. The following year she reinforced her impact in *Hell's Angels* by playing the floosie in James Cagney's classic gangster movie, *The Public Enemy* (1931; *Enemies of the People*) and appearing in Frank Capra's aptly titled comedy *Platinum Blonde* (1931).

In 1932 Harlow signed a contract with MGM, where she made a series of very popular films with Clark Gable. They had earlier appeared, both in supporting roles, in MGM's *The Secret Six* (1931), and went on to star in five films together. But first Harlow took the starring role in *Red-Headed Woman* (1932), which ran into trouble with the censors, receiving complaints from the Hays Office since Harlow's heroine never pays for her sins. It was also refused a certificate in Britain. This marked the beginning of her greatest period. *Red Dust* (1932), advertised with the line 'He treated her rough – and she loved it!', was the true beginning of her successful teaming with Gable, in a role originally intended for John Gilbert. This was followed by the all-star *Dinner at Eight* (1933), *Bombshell* (1933; *Blonde Bombshell*, another of her popular nicknames), a superb satire on Hollywood and her most undervalued film, and another film with Gable, *China Seas* (1935). She ran into trouble with the censors again in 1934, this time over the title of 'Born to be Kissed'. The censors insisted on a change, and so it became *100% Pure*, although it is probably better known as *The Girl from Missouri* (1934; *Eadie Was a Lady*). Her star continued to shine for the rest of her brief career, as she appeared in the popular all-star comedies *Wife Versus Secretary* (1936) and *Libeled Lady* (1937). Unfortunately her last movie, *Saratoga* (1937),

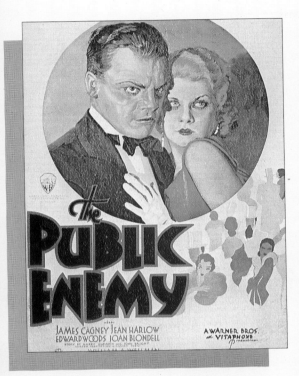

■ ■ ■

FAR LEFT
The Public Enemy (1931)
was an important early
film for Harlow, in which
she was perfectly cast
as James Cagney's
mistress, Gwen.

■ ■ ■

LEFT
Harlow's strong sex
appeal, which often
provoked the wrath of
the censors, is clearly
evident. By 1933 it had
put her among
America's top ten box
office stars.

■ ■ ■

again with Gable, is her dullest. The film was completed with a double after Harlow tragically died during production.

Aside from this impressive body of films, Harlow's personal life has also attracted plenty of attention. She was first married at 16, wrote a semi-erotic novel called *Today is Tonight* which MGM did its best to suppress, and entered into a second unsuccessful marriage with MGM producer Paul Bern. Bern committed suicide only two months after their wedding, the reasons for which have never been satisfactorily explained, although the most common theory concerns his impotence. His naked body was found in their bathroom where he had shot himself. Bern left behind a note which read, 'Unfortunately this is the only way to make good the frightful wrong I have done you, and to wipe out my abject humiliation'. He also added, 'You understand that last night was only a comedy'.

Harlow next married and quickly divorced leading cinematographer Hal Rossen, an Oscar

winner for his work on *The Garden of Allah* (1936).
Her final affair was with actor William Powell. She
became ill with a kidney disease soon after their
break up. Unfortunately her mother was a Christian
Scientist and attempted to cure her without
medicine. On 7 June 1937 Jean Harlow died from
uremic poisoning at the age of 26.

The fascination with Harlow continued long after
her death. She was obviously the inspiration for
Carroll Baker's character in *The Carpetbaggers*
(1964), while Baker also starred in one of two films
(the other featured Carol Lynley) called *Harlow*,

produced in 1965. Despite her tragic private life
and the heavy emphasis on her sexuality, Jean
Harlow's strength was comedy, rather like another
famous blonde in the 1950s.

Jean Harlow to Marie Dressler in Dinner at
Eight, *commenting on a book she had just read:*
'Do you know that the guy said that machinery
is going to take the place of every profession?'
'Oh, my dear, that's something you'll never
have to worry about.'

OTHER STARS 1930-1939

James Murray (1901–1936)

*James Murray spent most of the 1920s as an extra or
playing small roles before King Vidor chose him for
the lead in* The Crowd *(1928), a film which ranks
among the silent cinema's finest. Vidor wanted a
completely unknown face for the leading role of the
ordinary clerk who finds life hard in New York.
Murray also found life hard; he was soon relegated
to supporting roles and turned to alcohol. In 1936
his body was found in New York's Hudson River.*

Pearl White (1889–1938)

*Pearl White was the cinema's first serial queen,
proving a great hit in the early serials* The Perils of
Pauline *(1914) and* The Exploits of Elaine *(1914).
Her image is firmly fixed – tied to the railway tracks,
awaiting the last minute rescue by the handsome
hero – partly through the highly fictional biopic*
Perils of Pauline *(1947) starring Betty Hutton. She
continued acting into the 1920s, retiring from the
cinema in 1924.*

1908 ★ 1942

CAROLE LOMBARD

Carole Lombard was only in her early thirties when the plane carrying her on a war bond selling tour crashed near Las Vegas on 16 January 1942. Yet she had been a star for over a decade and in movies for more than 20 years. She was Hollywood's first civilian war casualty and her death was a tragic loss to Hollywood.

She was born Jane Alice Peters in Fort Wayne, Indiana, and made her movie debut, at the age of 12, playing a tomboy in Allan Dwan's *The Perfect Crime* (1921). Her debut came after she had been spotted by the director playing baseball with the local kids. In fact, according to Dwan, she was actually 'out there knocking hell out of the other kids, playing better baseball than they were'. Throughout her life Lombard noticeably preferred male company, as well as gaining a reputation for her colourful language. She went on to become one of Mack Sennett's bathing beauties and appeared in numerous routine movies throughout the '20s.

Her fortune changed when in 1931 she appeared in two films with William Powell, *Man of the World* and *Ladies' Man*, and they married the same year. The following year Lombard made her only film with future husband Clark Gable, *No Man of Her Own* (1932). She was to remain close friends with Powell after their short-lived marriage ended in 1933, starring with him again in the popular *My Man Godfrey* (1936). After the atypical *Supernatural* (1933), in which Lombard played a character possessed by the soul of a dead murderess, she had a big hit opposite George Raft in *Bolero* (1934) and then embarked on a string of classic comedies.

The first is perhaps the best, *Twentieth Century* (1934), a fast-paced comedy satirizing the

theatrical world, which builds up to a fine second half aboard the train of the title and features a splendidly over-the-top performance from John Barrymore. The role only came her way after being turned down by Miriam Hopkins. Next came her most underrated movie, *Hands Across the Table* (1935) opposite Fred MacMurray, followed by *My Man Godfrey* (1936). *My Man Godfrey* unfortunately does not quite live up to its reputation, but is certainly preferable to the June Allyson remake and won Lombard her only Oscar nomination. The following year she maintained these high standards with *True Confession* (1937), again with MacMurray and Barrymore, and the superb *Nothing Sacred* (1937), a bitter comedy worthy of Billy Wilder. This rare excursion into colour was later remade, with Jerry Lewis recreating the Lombard role.

Lombard next switched to melodrama, playing opposite James Stewart in *Made for Each Other* (1938) and Cary Grant in *In Name Only* (1939). The teaming with Grant, uniting two of Hollywood's most sophisticated stars, was effective enough to regret that they made no further films together. In 1939 she also married Gable, making them Hollywood's best known off-screen couple. Their

happy relationship was tragically cut short by Lombard's untimely death.

Carole Lombard reputedly turned down *His Girl Friday* (1940) during this period, but made amends by starring in Ernst Lubitsch's *To Be or Not to Be* (1942). *To Be or Not to Be* suffered accusations of tastelessness on its first release, as it was set in Warsaw, involved the Polish resistance and was a comedy. Today it is simply regarded as a classic, one of Lubitsch's finest films. Unfortunately it was Carole Lombard's last.

'They never would let me in the fight. I had to simper at the hero and scream with terror when the heavy came after me. They never would let me get in there and give the villain a good kick in the bustle.' – Carole Lombard on her dissatisfying early roles in The Films of Carole Lombard, *by Frederick W Ott.*

'She is and always will be a star, one we shall never forget, nor cease to be grateful for.' – Cable from President Roosevelt to Clark Gable on hearing of Lombard's death.

RIGHT
Carole Lombard on the set of *They Knew What They Wanted* (1940) with director Garson Karvin (left) and husband Clark Gable.

■ ■ ■

CHILDREN OF THE NIGHT – THE HORROR STARS

The horror genre, despite being so often maligned, has attracted some first-rate character actors, such as Laird Cregar and Victor Buono, although the genre undoubtedly has the capacity to be cruelly exploitive, as the case of Rondo Hatton clearly illustrates.

COLIN CLIVE
1898 ★ 1937

Two noted actors from Universal's Frankenstein series, Colin Clive and Dwight Frye, both suffered tragically early deaths. Colin Clive was descended from the famous Clive of India and had a spell at Sandhurst Royal Military Academy before a fractured knee put an end to any hopes of a military career. Instead, he turned to acting and gained his best notices for his performance as Captain Stanhope in *Journey's End* in 1929. Clive was the natural choice for the same role in the film version the following year. The director of both the stage and cinema versions was the great James Whale, who insisted on Clive for the role of Dr Henry Frankenstein in *Frankenstein* (1931) despite Universal wanting to cast Leslie Howard.

Clive gave an excellent performance, playing a driven man, often seeming on the brink of a nervous breakdown. By all accounts Clive himself was a strangely sensitive man, who often resorted to drink. According to his *Frankenstein* co-star David Manners, 'I knew he was a tormented man. There seemed to be a split in his personality: one side that was soft, kind and gentle; the other, a man who took to drink to hide from the world of his true nature'. Clive reprised his role in the even better sequel, *The Bride of Frankenstein* (1935), again directed by his friend James Whale, and starred in the

excellent *Mad Love* (1935; *The Hands of Orlac*). He was also successful away from the horror genre, but Clive's time in Hollywood was relatively short. Two years after these successes, in June 1937, he died from pulmonary tuberculosis.

DWIGHT FRYE
1899 ★ 1943

Dwight Frye was also popular on the stage, having been nominated one of Broadway's ten finest actors in the late 1920s. Following his stage success as a leading man he tried his luck in Hollywood, making a strong impression as the insane Renfield in *Dracula* (1930) and the hunchback Fritz in *Frankenstein* (1931). His fate was sealed. Frye found roles away from the horror genre increasingly rare. He was seen in *The Vampire Bat* (1933), *The Invisible Man* (1933), *The Bride of Frankenstein* (1935), *The Ghost of Frankenstein* (1942), *Frankenstein Meets the Wolf Man* (1943) and *Dead*

■ ■ ■
ABOVE
The Baron (Colin Clive) tracks down his monster (Boris Karloff) in *Frankenstein* (1931). The two reunited four years later for an even better sequel, *The Bride of Frankenstein* (1935).
■ ■ ■

Men Walk (1943), among others. However, many were small roles and, according to film historian Gregory William Mank, prior to the filming of *Ghost of Frankenstein*, Frye 'had been reduced to playing in a stag film as a voyeur hiding in the bushes, watching a nude volleyball game'. Frye was not to suffer such indignities much longer. He died from a heart attack on 7 November 1943.

LAIRD CREGAR
1916 ★ 1944

Laird Cregar was a large actor who played characters, usually heavies, older than his years. He made his debut in *Granny Get Your Gun* (1939) and came to attention with a supporting role in the thriller *I Wake Up Screaming* (1941; *Hot Spot*). He quickly capitalized on this success with further supporting roles in the Alan Ladd movie *This Gun for Hire* (1942), as a splendid larger-than-life

villain in the lavish Tyrone Power pirate movie *The Black Swan* (1942), and Lubitsch's comedy classic *Heaven Can Wait* (1943).

Following this string of striking supporting performances Cregar was in a position to command starring roles, and his first was Jack the Ripper in a sumptuous version of *The Lodger* (1944). Director John Brahm created a fine fantasy version of Victorian London and the film featured a splendid cast; Merle Oberon, George Sanders, Cedric Hardwicke and Sara Allgood. His follow up was the

similar *Hangover Square* (1944), with Cregar this time playing an unbalanced composer driven to murder. The film was again directed by Brahm from a screenplay by Barre Lyndon and surpassed *The Lodger* on all counts. Linda Darnell was a more effective female lead than Oberon and the film was even more extravagantly melodramatic. Unfortunately this was to be Cregar's final performance; he died from a heart attack after slimming for the role, aged only 28.

RONDO HATTON
1894 ★ 1946

In contrast, Rondo Hatton never had a major role in a quality production. Yet in fairness he was hardly the actor Cregar was. He was chosen for his roles purely on the basis of his deformed face, caused by a rare disease called acromegaly, which attacks the pituitary gland and results in a disfigured face, hands, and feet.

He languished in bit parts (*The Hunchback of Notre Dame*, 1939, being the only horror film) until he was cast by Universal as The Creeper in one of their Sherlock Holmes films, *The Pearl of Death* (1944). Not surprisingly, given his unusual appearance, Hatton made quite an impression, and over the next two years Hollywood exploited his deformity in a series of tawdry horror films. He was rarely given any dialogue in these movies.

He was cast in the serial *Raiders of Ghost City* (1944), *Jungle Captive* (1945), *House of Horrors* (1946; *Joan Medford is Missing*) and *The Spider Woman Strikes Back* (1946). The latter title character, played by Gale Sondergaard, had been resurrected from a film in Universal's Sherlock Holmes series. He finally played the title role in *The Brute Man* (1946), a film which so embarrassed Universal that they released it through the poverty row studio PRC. Hatton died on 2 February 1946, the diagnosis being coronary thrombosis caused by chronic myocarditis (inflamation of the heart). His death, like his fame, was due to acromegaly.

VICTOR BUONO
1938 ★ 1982

Victor Buono at 300 pounds (136 kilogrammes) was, like Cregar, another large character actor who made a strong impression in horror movies; he was nominated for an Oscar as Best Supporting Actor for his debut performance in *Whatever Happened to Baby Jane?* (1962).

Director Robert Aldrich also cast him in his next two pictures, *Four for Texas* (1963), and another Baby Jane style picture again starring Bette Davis, the underrated *Hush Hush Sweet Charlotte* (1964). In between these two movies Buono reinforced his position as a new horror star with *The Strangler* (1963). However, he never really fulfilled his potential, starring in a few minor horror vehicles, such as the abysmal *Strangler of Vienna* (1972; *The Mad Butcher* or *Meat is Meat*), *Moonchild* (1972) and *The Evil* (1978; *Cry Demon* and *The Force Beyond*). In addition, Buono wasted his talents in big budget '60s movies, like *The Silencers* (1966), and dismal television movies. He died in his California home in 1982.

ABOVE
Victor Buono in his first and best role, as Edwin Flagg in *Whatever Happened to Baby Jane?* (1962).

1893 ★ 1943

LESLIE HOWARD

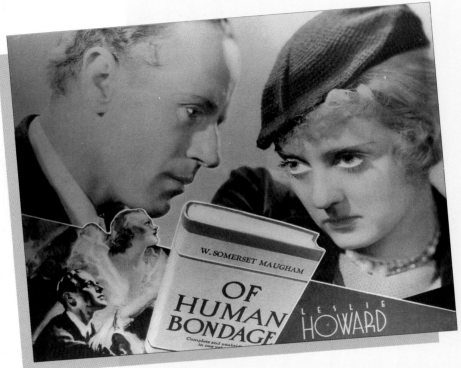

Like Carole Lombard, Leslie Howard was also a major star who died in a wartime plane crash, on 1 June 1943 over the Bay of Biscay. However, there the similarities end. Howard was hardly glamorous, was more interested in producing and directing, and epitomized Britishness, despite being half-Hungarian and Jewish. He was a fine actor, always capable of projecting intelligence, and used his voice to excellent effect, qualities he shared with two other British stars of the period, Ronald Colman and Robert Donat.

After working as a bank clerk and being invalided out of the army with severe shellshock during World War I, Leslie Howard took up acting, appearing in a few minor silent movies and having considerable success on the stage in both Britain

and the United States. However, his big break in the cinema did not come until 1930 with *Outward Bound*, a supernatural drama set on board an ocean liner on which all the passengers discover they are dead. A critical hit, appearing on both the *New York Times'* and National Board of Review's best of the year list, it established Howard as a major new film star. He reinforced this position with the romantic fantasy *Berkeley Square* (1933), for which he received an Oscar nomination, a version of W Somerset Maugham's *Of Human Bondage* (1934) opposite Bette Davis, and a return to Britain to star in Alexander Korda's *The Scarlet Pimpernel* (1934). The film was a huge hit, although it does not now compare favourably with Powell and Pressburger's later version of the same story, *The Elusive Pimpernel* (1950).

Howard did not abandon the stage during the 1930s, and appeared in New York in *The Petrified Forest* opposite Humphrey Bogart, whose name at this time meant little to the producers in

Leslie Howard

Hollywood. Not surprisingly, when Warners acquired the film rights they intended their leading gangster star, Edward G Robinson, to play the Bogart role, much to Howard's displeasure. Howard had promised Bogart that, should the play ever be adapted for the cinema, he would play Duke Mantee. He cabled Warners, insisting that if Bogart was not cast, then Howard would not appear in the picture. The rest is well known; the film helped establish Bogart's image and launched him on his film career (see page 37). The following year they appeared together again in the enjoyable comedy *Stand In* (1937) and, in 1952, nearly ten years after Howard's death, Bogart named his daughter Leslie Howard Bogart in recognition of the British star's support.

Meanwhile, Howard continued to star in prestige productions. In 1936 he was a rather elderly Romeo to Norma Shearer's less than youthful Juliet; he was the weak-willed Ashley Wilkes (a role he hated) in *Gone with the Wind* (1939); and starred opposite Ingrid Bergman in her first American picture, *Intermezzo* (1939; *Escape to Happiness*). He was also chosen to play Lawrence of Arabia in Alexander Korda's 1937 production, a film which was unfortunately never made. During this period Howard became more involved behind the camera. In 1938 he both co-directed, with Anthony Asquith, and starred in, a popular version of Bernard Shaw's *Pygmalion* (1938) in Britain. Despite receiving an Oscar nomination for his performance, the film has regrettably been overshadowed by the musical remake, *My Fair Lady* (1964).

Howard then moved back to Britain permanently, working on a series of excellent

■ ■ ■

BELOW
Possibly his best known role – and the one he enjoyed the least – Leslie Howard as Ashley Wilkes with Vivien Leigh as Scarlett O'Hara and Olivia de Havilland as Melanie in *Gone With The Wind* (1939).

■ ■ ■

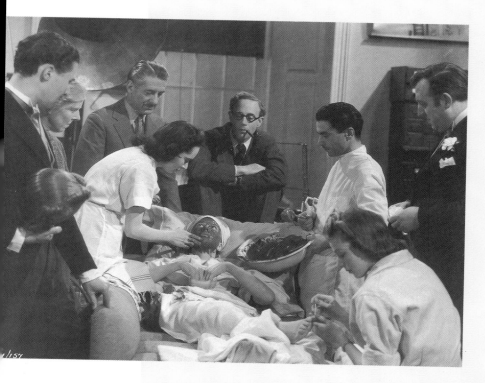

ABOVE
Leslie Howard (centre) first turned to directing with this successful adaptation of George Bernard Shaw's *Pygmalion*. He also took the lead role of Professor Higgins and was named Best Actor at the 1938 Venice Film Festival.

RIGHT
Howard was making propaganda movies during World War II and may have been involved in more secret war work. He and 16 fellow passengers died on 1st June 1943 when German aircraft shot down their passenger plane, returning from Lisbon to London.

Howard was now acting less and less, and in his last two years produced *The First of the Few* (1942; *Spitfire*), detailing R J Mitchell's (played by Howard) attempts to perfect the Spitfire; *The Gentle Sex* (1943), the story of seven ATS women; and *The Lamp Still Burns* (1943), focusing on wartime probationary nurses. The film world lost a potentially great director when Howard's plane was shot down while returning to London. He had been on a trip to Lisbon, prompted by government fears that Spain and Portugal might enter the war on the Axis' side. It is thought that the Germans believed that Churchill, who was returning from a conference in Algiers, was flying with Howard, although it is equally possible that Howard himself was the target.

'For as the Pimpernel concealed a strength and tenacity of purpose behind a flippant air, so did Howard disguise an art conceived in terms of hard work and perfect timing behind the casual understatement, the offhand approach, the quietly humorous habit of self-depreciation.' – The Times *obituary.*

'The brutality of the Germans was only matched by the stupidity of their agents. It is difficult to understand how anyone could imagine that with all the resources of Great Britain at my disposal I should have booked a passage in an unarmed and unescorted plane from Lisbon and flown home in broad daylight.' – Winston Churchill *on Howard's death.*

wartime propaganda pictures. He reworked one of his earlier hits, *The Scarlet Pimpernel*, as *Pimpernel Smith* (1941; *Mister V* or *The Fighting Pimpernel*), both directing and playing the lead role of a professor who rescues refugees from Nazi-occupied Europe, and took a cameo role in Powell and Pressburger's *49th Parallel* (1941; *The Invaders*). Powell and Pressburger, better known as The Archers, were the only filmmakers whose propaganda movies surpassed Howard's.

Leslie Howard Missing in Plane Shot Down by Nazis
3 WOMEN, 2 CHILDREN AMONG 17 LOST: SEARCH FOR RUBBER BOATS IN ROUGH SEA

CABLES from Lisbon last night confirmed that Mr. Leslie Howard, famous film actor and Brains Trust broadcaster, was among 17 passengers, who included three women and two children, British Overseas Airways aircraft which was among
between Portugal

THE CHARACTER ACTORS

Character actors are an essential part of Hollywood and the movies. Their names might not have been on the tip of everyone's tongue, but their faces were instantly recognizable and usually very welcome. The best could steal a film from the established star and rescue even the drabbest movie. These familiar supporting actors worked as a form of shorthand, playing the same roles time and time again, and so bringing an established character to the screen and saving the scriptwriter pages of dialogue. The character actors almost merit a separate volume. We can really only hope to scratch the surface here.

ROBERT BENCHLEY
1889 ★ 1945

Robert Benchley was almost a character star, appearing in his own series of comic shorts throughout his career. These included the famous *The Sex Life of the Polyp* (1928) and the 'How to . . .' series, one of which, *How to Sleep* (1935), won an Oscar as the year's Best Short. His comic timing was impeccable, evident in his success on radio, while he was also a celebrated humorous author. He enlivened many movies in supporting roles, memorably in the Hope-Crosby comedy *The Road to Utopia* (1945), René Clair's *I Married a Witch* (1942) and Hitchcock's *Foreign Correspondent* (1940). Benchley's style was that of the loveable bumbler, often giving rambling comic speeches, and his death through cerebral haemorrhage robbed Hollywood of one of its most distinctive talents.

CHARLES BUTTERWORTH
1896 ★ 1946

On the other hand, Charles Butterworth, a close friend of Benchley's, was a more conventional

character actor. A face that everyone would recognize, but a name only the film buffs would remember. His appearance in a film was nevertheless welcomed by cinemagoers everywhere. He often played the upper class twit, or a rather timid character, and appeared in a number of classic movies. He had started on Broadway, made his Hollywood debut in 1930 and can be seen in *Love Me Tonight* (1932), *Ruggles of Red Gap* (1935) and *The Magnificent Obsession* (1935). He died from head injuries after his car skidded into a lamp post.

PAUL DOUGLAS
1907 ★ 1959

Paul Douglas was certainly a star character actor. Following his stage success in *Born Yesterday*, he made a strong impression in his first film, *A Letter to Three Wives* (1949), which was nominated for an Oscar as the year's Best Picture. Burly Paul Douglas soon established himself playing gruff,

frequently powerful, characters, often concealing a soft heart. He played in major films, such as *The Big Lift* (1949) starring Montgomery Clift, the acclaimed thrillers *Panic in the Streets* (1950) and *Fourteen Hours* (1951), and the boardroom melodrama *Executive Suite* (1953). But his best role was found far from Hollywood, in the classic Ealing comedy *The Maggie* (1953; *High and Dry*), filmed on location on the west coast of Scotland. He played an American businessman desperate to get his cargo to a Scottish island but who is constantly outmanœuvred by Alex Mackenzie's tugboat owner. Throughout the remainder of the '50s Douglas continued to appear in some first-rate movies. He would no doubt have featured in many more had he not died of a heart attack, at the age of 52, while preparing for a leading role in Billy Wilder's *The Apartment* (1960).

EVERETT SLOANE
1909 ★ 1965

An even more respected character actor was Everett Sloane, who was a member of Orson Welles' repertory company. He made his debut in the pivotal role of Bernstein in the classic *Citizen Kane* (1941). He followed this performance with another part in a Welles film, the often ignored *Journey Into Fear* (1942), an enjoyable thriller based on the Eric Ambler novel. Cinemagoers had to wait another six years for Sloane's third appearance on screen. His corrupt, deceitful Arthur Bannister in Welles' superb *The Lady from Shanghai* (1948) proved worth the wait. The '50s saw him in some excellent movies. He appeared in Brando's debut film *The Men* (1950), the first-rate Bogart thriller *The Enforcer* (1951), the boardroom melodrama *Patterns* (1956), and the boxing movie *Somebody Up There Likes Me* (1956). Unfortunately, they did not last and the '60s saw mostly supporting roles in routine comedies. He committed suicide on 6 August 1965, with an overdose of sleeping pills.

FRED CLARK
1914 ★ 1968

Fred Clark, often seen chewing on a cigar, was an instantly recognizable figure with his balding head. He was most at home in comedies, appearing with Bob Hope in *The Lemon Drop Kid* (1951) and the all-star *How to Marry a Millionaire* (1953). Clark was also seen in Billy Wilder's classic *Sunset Boulevard* (1950) as the movie producer Sheldrake. By the mid-1960s, however, Clark was consistently acting in exploitation movies, with such fantastic titles as *Dr Goldfoot and the Bikini Machine* (1966) and *I Sailed to Tahiti with an All Girl Crew* (1968). His talents would have easily transferred to the television sitcom, but he died when he was only 54, suffering from a liver ailment.

OTHER STARS 1940-1949

Lupe Velez (1908–1944)

Lupe Velez was known to most cinemagoers as 'The Mexican Spitfire', the name of the title character in a series of eight movies Velez made for RKO opposite comic actor Leon Errol between 1939 and 1943. It was a name Velez reputedly lived up to in her private life. Earlier she had appeared in such major productions as The Gaucho *(1927), opposite Douglas Fairbanks, and Cecil B de Mille's* The Squaw Man *(1931; The White Man), and married the cinema's most famous Tarzan, Johnny Weissmuller. With her career on a definite downward spiral, as well as being pregnant and in debt, Velez committed suicide on 15 December 1944.*

Carole Landis (1919–1948)

Carole Landis worked as an extra before she gained more prominent roles in the Hal Roach movies One Million BC *(1940; Man and His Mate),* Turnabout *(1940) and* Topper Returns *(1941). She continued to work steadily in routine American and British films throughout the '40s until she committed suicide in 1948 with an overdose of sleeping pills. Her death was the result of her love for film star Rex Harrison, who refused to leave his wife Lilli Palmer.*

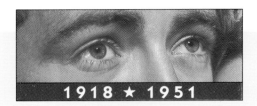

1918 ★ 1951

ROBERT WALKER

'Some people are better off dead. Like your wife and my father, for instance.' This statement could only come from Bruno Anthony, talking to dull tennis player Guy Haines in Alfred Hitchcock's classic thriller *Strangers on a Train* (1951). Bruno dominates Walker's film career – this slightly effeminate, egotistical, rather charming character being by far his best role – in the same manner that Bruno dominates the film. Nobody is interested in the bland Farley Granger, all eyes are watching Bruno as he proceeds to murder Guy's wife and expects Guy to kill his father in return.

Nothing in Walker's career could really have prepared anyone for his extraordinary performance in *Strangers on a Train*. He was born in the heart of Mormon country, in Salt Lake City, Utah, and made his film debut in the innocuous college comedy *Winter Carnival* (1939). Walker, signed to an MGM contract, played supporting roles in their films throughout the early 1940s, most notably in a trio of wartime propaganda hits; *Bataan* (1943), *Thirty Seconds Over Tokyo* (1944) and, for David O Selznick, the all-star *Since You Went Away* (1944), which also featured his wife Jennifer Jones. He showed real promise in Vincente Minnelli's first non-musical, *The Clock* (1945; *Under the Clock*), which was also a rare dramatic success for Judy Garland. The story was set over a 24-hour period, as a young soldier on leave (Walker) falls in love with, and then marries, a young New Yorker he meets at Grand Central Station. Featuring fine supporting performances – James Gleason, Lucile Gleason, Keenan Wynn – and, unusually for the time, scenes shot on location in New York, the film impressed the critics and still holds up well today.

Walker appeared with Garland again the next year in *Till the Clouds Roll By* (1946), with Walker playing composer Jerome Kern, although the film was nowhere near the success of *The Clock*.

The next few years offered only routine roles, and it was during this period that Walker, a heavy drinker, was arrested for drunk driving, divorced from actress Jennifer Jones and became ill with a nervous disorder. In 1948 he married Barbara Ford, daughter of director John Ford, but the marriage only lasted five weeks. With the exception of *Strangers on a Train* the films remained ordinary and he died from respiratory failure during the making of the anti-communist film *My Son John* (1952), having been given sedatives to calm an emotional outburst. He had been drinking and the mixture proved fatal.

■ ■ ■
BELOW
Undoubtedly Robert Walker's (right) finest hour and a half, as the delightfully evil Bruno Anthony opposite Farley Granger as Guy Haines in Hitchcock's *Strangers on a Train* (1951).
■ ■ ■

'I basically felt inadequate, unwanted and unloved since I was born. I was always trying to make an escape from life. I was an aggressive little character, but what nobody knew but me was my badness was only a cover-up for a basic lack of self-confidence, that I really was more afraid than frightening.' – Robert Walker in Star-Crossed: The Story of Robert Walker and Jennifer Jones.

'He never talked about the future, since the future he had once envisioned had been so unmercifully destroyed, but I never saw him in a suicidal mood. Never. Bob was living – "existing" would be a more accurate description – one day at a time.' – Jim Henaghan on Robert Walker after Jennifer Jones had left him for producer David O Selznick in Star-Crossed: The Story of Robert Walker and Jennifer Jones.

■ ■ ■

LEFT
Robert Walker and Judy Garland in a publicity still for *The Clock* (1945), which made both The National Board of Review and *Time* magazine's 'Ten Best Films' list for 1945.

■ ■ ■

1913 ★ 1952

JOHN GARFIELD

John Garfield was a major star from the time he appeared in *Four Daughters* (1938) until his death 14 years later, but he has since been criminally neglected. This is surprising, since he had all the makings of a cult star. Garfield had a rebellious image, was a fine actor, appeared in some classic '40s thrillers, was hounded by the House Un-American Activities Committee for suspected left wing sympathies and died tragically young. Such is the stuff that cult heroes are made of. Except, it seems, for John Garfield.

He made his movie debut as an extra in *Footlight Parade* (1933). Prophetically the picture was produced by Warner Brothers, where Garfield was to be such a success. His style suited Warners, home to Bogart, Robinson, Cagney and Raft. He had a tough façade, intelligence, a hint of vulnerability and a forceful style of acting. But

movie success was still five years away. In the meantime he joined New York's left wing, avant-garde Group Theatre, which boasted such talent as Clifford Odets, Lee Strasberg, Franchot Tone and Elia Kazan. This was invaluable experience, shaping both his acting and his political views. Garfield remained with the Group until his departure for Hollywood in 1938.

His first major film role, that of the doomed Mickey Borden in *Four Daughters*, made him a star. *Four Daughters* remains a classic family melodrama, later remade as *Young at Heart* (1954) with Frank Sinatra in the Garfield role, and was a popular hit. It also earned Garfield an Oscar nomination in the Best Supporting Actor category. Given such a reaction Warners could hardly keep him out of the proposed sequel. But there remained one problem; the Garfield character had been killed in *Four Daughters*. The simple response was to remake the picture, call it *Daughters Courageous* (1939) and use virtually the same cast. It was again popular, but, as is usually the case, not as good.

During the early 1940s Garfield confirmed his star status, playing supporting roles in two major productions – *Juarez* (1939) and *The Sea Wolf* (1941) – and appearing in a string of ordinary starring vehicles. This was to be the situation for the next few years, Garfield finding himself starring in films which evoked memories of better movies. *Between Two Worlds* (1944) was a remake of *Outward Bound* (1930), *Castle on the Hudson* (1940; *Years without Days*) had earlier been made as *20,000 Years in Sing, Sing* (1932) and *The Fallen Sparrow* (1943) was reminiscent of *The Maltese Falcon* (1941), with a flag taking the place of the black bird.

In 1946 he landed the lead role in *The Postman Always Rings Twice* (1946), turning in a fine performance opposite Lana Turner. It is certainly the best American version of James Cain's novel. It was also the first of five excellent films he was to make over the next three years. In 1947 he appeared with Joan Crawford in the full-blooded melodrama *Humoresque* (1947) and made what is, alongside *Raging Bull* (1980), the best boxing movie, *Body and Soul* (1947). It was the first film for his own production company, Enterprise Productions. He received a well-deserved Oscar nomination for his performance as a boxer determined to succeed at any cost but who, finally, refuses to throw an important fight. A familiar tale, perhaps, but superbly told here. The script was by Abraham Polonsky, who was also a victim of the anti-communist witch-hunt which scarred Hollywood during the 1950s. However, before his blacklisting Polonsky was to direct Garfield in his best film, *Force of Evil* (1948). Like *Body and Soul*, *Force of Evil* was an atmospheric tale of corruption, this time focussing on the numbers racket. It was brilliantly shot on location in New York and benefited from a fine supporting performance by Thomas Gomez, playing Garfield's unsuccessful brother, seemingly in a permanent sweat. Between the two Polonsky films Garfield took a supporting role in Elia Kazan's *Gentleman's Agreement* (1947), which, for its time, was a strong attack on anti-semitism. Garfield's role was little more than an extended cameo, but the subject was obviously close to his heart – he was himself Jewish.

He continued to star in good, although not outstanding, pictures, while also turning down the male lead in *A Streetcar Named Desire* (1951). Then in 1951 he was called to appear in front of the House Un-American Activities Committee. He had been chosen because of his background with the left wing Group Theatre, his own left wing sympathies and his wife's active support of a number of left wing causes. The Committee wanted him to confirm people already named as communists. He refused. He also resisted a second appearance, and so was effectively blacklisted from working in Hollywood. This pressure certainly contributed to Garfield's fatal heart attack on 20 May 1952.

'As an actor Garfield was the darling of the romantic rebels – beautiful, enthusiastic, rich with the know-how of street intelligence. He had passion and a lyrical sadness that was the essence of the role he created.' – Director Abraham Polonsky in The Films of John Garfield, *by Howard Gelman.*

■ ■ ■
BELOW
Garfield at his peak, in the superb boxing drama *Body and Soul* (1947). In 1952 he played another boxer, this time on stage in *Golden Boy*.
■ ■ ■

1931 ★ 1955

JAMES DEAN

James Dean starred in only three movies. He had
bit parts in a further four. Yet he is still the
subject of mass adoration, a teen icon the world
over. It is almost certain Dean would not have
received this attention had he not died so young.
Equally doubtful is his range as an actor, as Dean's
mediocre performance in his last movie, *Giant*
(1956), hints. But that is hardly the point. His early
death ensured that Dean and Jim Stark, his
character from *Rebel without a Cause* (1955),
became one and the same for millions of teenagers.
It also ensured that, with the exception of Monroe,
more words have been written about him than any
other film star. His image is also reproduced almost
as frequently as Monroe's.

James Byron Dean was born on 8 February 1931
in Marion, Indiana, his middle name supposedly
coming from the 19th-century romantic poet Lord
Byron. He was brought up in Fairmont, Indiana,
mainly by his aunt and uncle after his mother's
death from cancer in 1940. By the age of 16 Dean
had taken to the stage, appearing in school
productions. His other interests as a youngster
included sport, especially baseball and basketball.
Dean's first professional performance came in late
1950, somewhat ignominiously, in a Pepsi-Cola
commercial.

By 1951, Dean was getting small roles on radio,
television and film, making his movie debut in the
Sam Fuller war movie *Fixed Bayonets* (1951).
Unfortunately his one line of dialogue was cut.
Nevertheless, further bit roles followed, in the
Dean Martin and Jerry Lewis comedy *Sailor Beware*
(1952), Douglas Sirk's *Has Anybody Seen My Gal?*
(1952) and the John Wayne movie *Trouble along the
Way* (1953). The following two years were spent in
television and theatre work. During this time he
won his first leading role on Broadway, in *See the
Jaguar*, which opened on 3 December 1952. It
closed three days later.

His luck really changed when he landed the role
of Cal Trask in *East of Eden* (1955), beating
Montgomery Clift to the part at the insistence of
director Elia Kazan and winning an Oscar
nomination into the bargain. This critically
respected movie, based on a novel by John
Steinbeck, tells the story of Cal and his brother
Aaron, who discover their father's lie about their
supposedly dead mother; she is found working as a
madam in a brothel. The film focuses on Cal's
resentment of his father, who he believes loves his
brother far more than him. It is a tale of confused
youth, family oppression, rejection and the search

TRASH STARS

MARIA MONTEZ

1920 ★ 1951

Throughout America's war years Maria Montez, whose real name was the even more exotic Maria Africa Vidal de Santo Silas, starred in a series of highly popular fantasy movies for Universal Pictures. Their mixture of colour, fantasy, revealing (for the time at least) costumes, humour and fantasy provided the perfect antidote to the hardships of World War II.

Montez seems to have been drawn to such films from the first, one of her early appearances being in the comedy *The Invisible Woman* (1941), a spin-off from Universal's long-running Invisible Man series. (Worse was to come for the Invisible Man; he had yet to meet Abbott and Costello!) Although a distinctly minor role, she next landed the lead in an adaptation of Edgar Allan Poe's *The Mystery of Marie Roget* (1942) and, the film that really launched her career, *Arabian Nights* (1942). This is the archetypal Montez vehicle: a colourful fantasy adventure, with an injection of cornball humour, played with great vigour and, above all, a sense of fun. The other chief ingredient of a Montez film was the cast, usually featuring Jon Hall as her leading man, with support coming from the young Sabu and a splendid array of Hollywood character actors. In *Arabian Nights* it was Thomas Gomez, Billy Gilbert (the voice of Sneezy in Disney's *Snow White* (1937), and long-time foil for Laurel and Hardy), Shemp Howard (of The Three Stooges) and villainous Turhan Bey, who was later the romantic lead in *Sudan* (1945). The supporting cast is certainly a fundamental part of these films' enduring popularity, alongside their new found camp appeal.

The series continued with *White Savage* (1943; *White Captive*), a South Seas island adventure

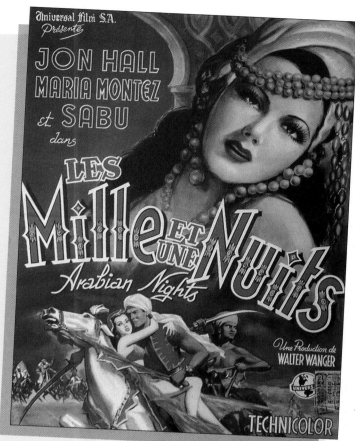

featuring crooks and shark hunters, *Cobra Woman* (1944), featuring the same location, only this time enlivened with snake worshippers and the inevitable volcano, *Ali Baba and the Forty Thieves* (1943), and *Gypsy Wildcat* (1944), which took place in Transylvania to make use of the sets from Universal's Frankenstein series. However, when the series resumed after the war, the time was wrong. The Betty Grable musicals and Maria Montez movies were rejected for the darker pleasures of the film noir. But for a while they still kept coming, Montez starring with husband Jean-Pierre Aumont in *Song of Scheherezade* (1947). They finally ground to a halt with *Siren of Atlantis* (1948) and Montez moved to France with her husband. Three years later, on 7 September 1951, she had a heart attack while taking a bath. The three hours spent trying to revive her through artificial respiration proved futile.

LEFT
Arabian Nights (1942), the archetypal Maria Montez movie, was amazingly nominated for two Oscars (for the photography and the music).

RIGHT
George Reeves in his
most famous role, as
Superman in *Superman
and the Mole Men*
(1951). The film later
turned up in the
television series as a
two-part adventure
called 'Unknown
People'.

GEORGE REEVES

1914 ★ 1959

George Reeves' fame was far shorter lived. The 6ft 2in (1.9m) actor made his debut in a small role in *Gone With the Wind* (1939), which he followed with supporting roles in entertaining hokum like *Jungle Goddess* (1948), *Jungle Jim* (1948) and a host of B westerns. His moment of glory finally came when he was cast as Superman by Sam Katzman, a producer of exploitation quickies who gave the world the Jungle Jim series, Bill Haley in *Rock Around the Clock* (1956) and two Superman serials in the late 1940s. Reeves first appeared in the role with which his name is now synonymous in *Superman and the Mole Men* (1951), a 67-minute B movie. This was rapidly followed by the television series, which firmly established Reeves as Superman in the public eye. The series proved exceptionally popular and ran for 104 episodes in the mid-'50s. In fact Reeves became so strongly associated with the man of steel and his alter ego Clark Kent that it was difficult for him to secure any other roles. So disheartened did Reeves become that, after the series was cancelled, he committed suicide. He shot himself in the head on 16 June 1959.

In 1944 Harvard Lampoon nominated Maria Montez as one of the three worst discoveries of the year. However, she was in good company. One of the other nominees was Frank Sinatra!

1899 ★ 1957

HUMPHREY BOGART

Humphrey Bogart is perhaps the archetypal Hollywood star. He is all things to all people. Both a cult symbol and a popular mainstream star, a forerunner of the modern anti-hero and lead in many golden era Hollywood productions, his appeal shows no sign of diminishing for young, old, nostalgia buffs and film students alike. Not bad for an actor who appeared as a child model on tins of baby food and was typecast on Broadway as the young lead who bounds through the French windows and shouts, 'Anyone for tennis?'

The Bogart character began to take shape on 7 January 1935, when he made his first of 181 performances as the gangster Duke Mantee in Robert Sherwood's play *The Petrified Forest*. The film version was to take Bogart to Hollywood (see page 23), although it was not for the first time. He had made his movie debut in 1930, and appeared in a number of films without making any impression on the audience. But this time was different. He had a part worth playing. It was to typecast him again, but this time as a vicious gangster in a series of movies for the studio with which his name is almost synonymous, Warner Brothers.

During the late 1930s Bogart was exceptionally busy. There were supporting roles in prestige productions, most memorably as Baby Face Martin in William Wyler's *Dead End* (1937), a story of life in the New York slums. Then there were the numerous films where Bogart played second fiddle to Cagney and Robinson, often as the vicious gangster with no redeeming features whose cowardice is exposed just before the climax. Into this category fall the gangster classics *Angels with Dirty Faces* (1938) and *The Roaring Twenties* (1939), as well as the neglected comedy *Brother*

Orchid (1940), which features crooked Edward G Robinson hiding out in a monastery. And finally there were the starring roles in the numerous B movies and programmers, which all the major studios churned out.

Among Bogart's late '30s films are also a fair share of embarrassments. He looked slightly uncomfortable in the westerns *The Oklahoma Kid* (1939) and *Virginia*

HUMPHREY BOGART · MARY ASTOR

A WARNER BR
FIRST NATION
PICTURE

the Maltese Falcon

ABOVE
'I won't play the sap for you' – Bogart as Sam Spade and Mary Astor as the manipulative Brigid O'Shaughnessy in *The Maltese Falcon* (1941).

City (1940) and fought a losing battle with an Irish accent as the horse trainer in the Bette Davis weepie, *Dark Victory* (1939), but surpassing all others was *The Return of Dr X* (1939). Bogart had been cast as the lead, Doctor Xavier, as a punishment by Warner Brothers for refusing parts he had considered inferior. And strong punishment it was, too. Bogart looked ridiculous with a silver streak down the middle of his hair and, instead of provoking chills, can only elicit laughter from a modern audience. It would perhaps seem slightly less risible if the image of Bogart as Sam Spade, Rick Blaine, Philip Marlowe et al was not now so firmly established.

Bogart's first important break since *The Petrified Forest* (1936) came in the early '40s. In fact it was a series of breaks, as other Warner Brothers stars turned down the roles that were to make Bogart famous. First came *High Sierra* (1941), the story of a convict's last, fateful heist, which George Raft turned down, supposedly because he was superstitious about dying on screen. Edward G Robinson and Paul Muni also rejected the part. But the film which really established the Bogart character was *The Maltese Falcon* (1941), another film Raft turned down, on this occasion because he

did not wish to work with a first time director. The director was John Huston, who also wrote the screenplay, worked with Bogart on a further four films, and was responsible for many outstanding movies. The character of Sam Spade is essential to an understanding of Bogart's appeal: independent, equally capable with a gun or the leading lady, cynical, loyal, possessing a sense of humour and a man with his own strict code of honour who is also perfectly at home in the criminal underworld.

The Bogart myth was finally completed by Rick Blaine, the leading character in *Casablanca* (1942), which added vulnerability to the mixture. For many this is the perfect Hollywood film, but nothing could have seemed more unlikely during production. Ingrid Bergman was uncertain whether she would walk away with Bogart or the dull freedom fighter played by Paul Henreid, since the script was still being written as filming progressed. But the casting was faultless (Claude Rains, Peter Lorre, Sydney Greenstreet in supporting roles), the technicians were Warners' finest, and the film's release most timely, coinciding with the Casablanca Conference of Anglo-American leaders. The film also brought Bogart his first Oscar nomination.

The film was originally cast with Ann Sheridan, Ronald Reagan and Dennis Morgan in the leads, which would have been disastrous. The success of the film essentially lies with the cast and crew, not the story, as one look at the dreadful Charles Bronson rehash *Caboblanco* (1981) or the David Soul television series will confirm.

The Bogart myth was further fuelled by his private life. He was a notable drinker ('The trouble with the world is that everybody in it is three drinks behind'), had a much publicized stormy third marriage to actress Mayo Methot (the 'Battling Bogarts', as they were known in the press, appeared together in *Marked Woman* (1937), and provided the press with almost as many good quotes as

Marilyn Monroe. Backed up by his run-ins with Warner Brothers over the roles he was given, the on-screen Bogart became, for many people, the off-screen Bogart as well. Perhaps Bogart began to believe it as well, as Hollywood restaurateur Dave Chasen claimed: 'Bogart's a hell of a nice guy until 11.30pm. After that he thinks he's Bogart.'

Bogart was now at the top of his profession, a position he would maintain until his death 15 years later with a string of superb films and fine performances. In the mid-1940s there were the four films with Lauren Bacall, who became his fourth wife after making her movie debut opposite him in *To Have and Have Not* (1945). Can there be any film fan who does not recognize Bacall's famous line to Bogart – 'You know how to whistle don't you, Steve, just put your lips together and blow'? This film was actually surpassed by their next movie together, *The Big Sleep* (1946), with Bogart making a perfect Philip Marlowe. The story was so complex that reputedly even author Raymond Chandler was unsure who killed the chauffeur. The screen crackled with some fairly explicit dialogue for the period and Bogart and Bacall established themselves as one of the cinema's great partnerships. Two more films followed, *Dark*

Passage (1947) and *Key Largo* (1948). However, at the time John Huston's *The Treasure of the Sierra Madre* (1948) gained Bogart more attention. While this tale of greed is certainly a fine movie, it perhaps seems just a touch too self-important today. The decade drew to a close with Bogart forming his own film company, Santana.

The '50s were equally bright, beginning with Nicholas Ray's cult movie *In a Lonely Place* (1950), which, despite a growing reputation, remains his most underrated film. The story of a Hollywood scriptwriter suspected of murder, this is an excellent study of violence. The following year came the ever-popular *The African Queen* (1951), which brought Bogart his only Oscar. The teaming with Katharine Hepburn, which at first must have seemed an unlikely pairing, proved to be inspired. Good roles continued to be offered to Bogart – *Beat the Devil* (1953), *The Caine Mutiny* (1954), *We're No Angels* (1954) – and showed no signs of subsiding when, despite a hard fight, he died from cancer in January 1957.

Bogart was not too happy with his early movies: 'In my last 34 pictures I was shot in 12, electrocuted or hanged in 8, and a jailbird in 9. I was the Little Lord Fauntleroy of the lot.'

■ ■ ■
ABOVE
The perfect team of Bogart and Bacall in their best movie, *The Big Sleep* (1946), which effortlessly eclipses the awful 1977 remake starring Robert Mitchum.
■ ■ ■

■ ■ ■
LEFT
Bogart finally won his Oscar for his performance as Charlie Allnut in *The African Queen* (1951), in which he was memorably teamed with Katharine Hepburn.
■ ■ ■

1909 ★ 1959

ERROL FLYNN

It is difficult to imagine that the wasted, dishevelled, overweight 50-year-old star of the desultory *Cuban Rebel Girls* (1959) had created such a strong impression as the romantic, swashbuckling Captain Blood, Robin Hood and the Earl of Essex. Millions of women around the world – and by all accounts a good many in Hollywood as well – fell for his dashing charm. But a lifetime of over-indulgence took its toll, as it had for his drinking partner John Barrymore in the early '40s.

Tasmanian-born Flynn told his own story in the highly colourful *My Wicked, Wicked Ways*, with tales of prospecting for gold in New Guinea and his life at sea. How much is true and how much benefited from poetic licence is almost immaterial. The important fact is that Errol Flynn was as large a character off screen as on.

He was signed by studio head Jack Warner after his appearance in the British movie *Murder at Monte Carlo* (1934) and almost immediately created a sensation in the title role of *Captain Blood* (1935), which had originally been intended for Robert Donat. While the production seems less impressive today, particularly when compared to *The Sea Hawk* (1940), the enthusiasm still shows through and Olivia de Havilland, Basil Rathbone and Lionel Atwill provide excellent support. The film featured in the top 20 box office hits of 1936, was nominated for an Oscar as Best Picture (losing out to *Mutiny on the Bounty*, 1935) and established Flynn as a Hollywood star. It marked the beginning of a five-year golden period for Flynn, usually in association with director Michael Curtiz, leading lady Olivia de Havilland and the burly character actor Alan Hale.

The second half of the '30s saw Flynn as star of *The Charge of the Light Brigade* (1936), *The Prince and the Pauper* (1937), the World War I aerial action movie *The Dawn Patrol* (1938), Warner Brothers' finest western, *Dodge City* (1939), and an unhappy – at least off-screen – teaming with Bette Davis in *The Private Lives of Elizabeth and Essex* (1939; *Elizabeth the Queen*). However, towering above all these is *The Adventures of Robin Hood* (1938), superbly shot in Technicolor and featuring a perfect supporting cast: treacherous Basil Rathbone as Sir Guy of Gisbourne, oily Claude Rains as Prince John, virginal Olivia de Havilland as Maid Marian, jovial Alan Hale as Little John and portly Eugene Pallette playing Friar Tuck. It not surprisingly cost $2 million, Warners' most expensive production at the time, but after over 50 years remains the equal of any action movie

REBEL WITHOUT A CAUSE

Rebel Without a Cause (1955) is the seminal 'Hollywood Heaven' film. Not only does the film's star, James Dean, epitomize the 'live fast, die young' mentality, but the whole mythology surrounding *Rebel* is imbued with this radical stance. This, on analyzing the plot, is perhaps surprising. The alienated trio of Dean, Natalie Wood and Sal Mineo might fight against a claustrophobic, uncaring society, but they then end up forming their own version of the family. And the film has definite sexist undertones, with Jim Stark (the James Dean character) being ashamed that his mother should be stronger than his father.

But it is the images and performers that audiences remember, not any underlying ideology. There's the famous chicken run, Jim Stark's arrest for being drunk and disorderly as the film opens, the leather-jacketed juvenile delinquents, the gangs, the knife fight between Jim and Buzz. The list seems endless. The rebel image of James Dean (see pages 32–34) is firmly stamped on the mind of virtually every western teenager and cult star and Natalie Wood (see pages 80–82) was also to die young. The cast is completed by every cult movie fan's favourite psycho, Dennis Hopper, and two actors who lived tragically short lives: Nick Adams (see page 50) and Sal Mineo. Even director Nicholas Ray has a cult following for films like *They Live by Night* (1948), *In a Lonely Place* (1950) and *Party Girl* (1958).

New York-born Sal Mineo (1939–1976) received an Oscar nomination for his performance as Plato in *Rebel Without a Cause*, but unfortunately seems to have subsequently been neglected by the film's fans. However, during the 1950s Mineo's career looked promising. He had made his debut in the '30s gangster movie *Six Bridges to Cross* (1955) and went on to appear again with Dean in the ponderous *Giant* (1956). In 1956 he was also named among the

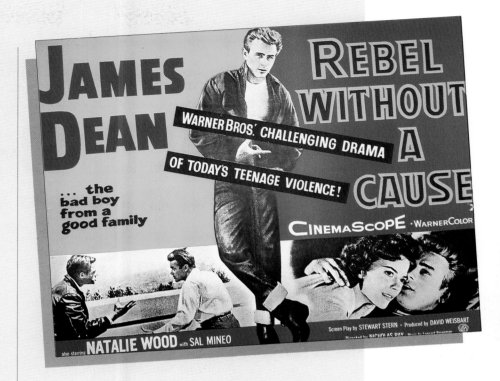

ten Stars of Tomorrow by American film exhibitors in their annual poll, along with *Rebel* co-star Natalie Wood (hardly a brave choice, as she had made her movie debut 13 years earlier!). He would have supported Dean again if Dean had lived to make *Somebody Up There Likes Me* (1956), the story of world boxing champion Rocky Graziano. Paul

■ ■ ■
BELOW
The three leads of *Rebel Without A Cause*, Sal Mineo, James Dean and Natalie Wood, each fated for a tragically early death.
■ ■ ■

Dorothy Hamill Wins Gold for U.S.
Sports Magazine, Sec. C.

LOS ANGELES EVENING AND SUNDAY
HERALD ⚏ EXAMINER
United Press International • Associated Press • Dow Jones
CLASSIFIED ADVERTISING Richmond 8-4111
All Other Calls Richmond 8-1212
VOL. CV NO. 320 FRIDAY, FEBRUARY 13, 1976 PRICE 15 CENTS

SUNSET
RACE RESULTS
COMPLETE STOCKS

SAL MINEO MURDERED
Actor Ambushed in W. Hollywood

Newman successfully took over the role intended for Dean. Mineo rounded out the decade with *Exodus* (1960) and a second Oscar nomination as Best Supporting Actor.

However, during the '60s Mineo's career went into rapid decline. His image was firmly linked to the rock'n'roll era of the '50s and found no place in the surf-happy, squeaky-clean early '60s. On 12 February 1976 Sal Mineo was found, stabbed and dying, in the alley near his Hollywood home. He had been making his way home after rehearsals for a new play called *PS Your Cat is Dead.* The reasons behind his murder were never established robbery having been ruled out as Mineo's wallet was still on his body.

'We never became lovers, but we could have.' – *Sal Mineo on James Dean.*

Dust (1932), in a role originally intended for John Gilbert. It was an energetic sex melodrama and established the partnership with Jean Harlow. They went on to make a series of popular, rollicking action-comedy-dramas until Harlow's death in 1937 (see pages 14–16).

But his two greatest successes of this period were made without Harlow. First came a low-key comedy, adapted from a short story called *Night Bus* for the then relatively minor studio, Columbia. The male lead was first offered to another MGM star, Robert Montgomery. He was not interested. MGM, who owed Columbia a star from an earlier deal, agreed to loan out Gable, partly because he was in studio head Louis B Mayer's bad books over his protests at being typecast. The female role proved equally difficult to fill, with Myrna Loy, Margaret Sullavan, Miriam Hopkins and Constance Bennett all turning it down before Claudette Colbert accepted the part. However, under director Frank Capra's magic touch *Night Bus* turned into the classic *It Happened One Night* (1934) and became the first film to win Oscars for all the principal participants – best picture, director, actor, actress and writer. This despite the general disinterest shown by the critics on its initial release. It was actually the audiences who loved the simple story of a spoilt runaway heiress falling in love with a slightly arrogant reporter on a bus journey across country. It remains one of the finest American comedies. Classic scenes abound. For instance, who could forget Colbert's legs proving mightier than Gable's thumb, despite all his boasting, when it comes to hitching a lift? *It Happened One Night* also illustrates the cinema's influence during the '30s. When Gable removed his shirt to reveal he wore no vest, thousands of men followed suit, resulting in a massive slump in vest sales.

The second great film was *Mutiny on the Bounty* (1935), which still eclipses both the Marlon Brando and Mel Gibson remakes. Gable is perfect as

Hollywood's idea of Fletcher Christian, radiating integrity, honesty, strength and independence. It is a measure of Gable's skills as a film actor that he is never overshadowed by Charles Laughton's excellent performance as Captain Bligh. He was again nominated for an Oscar and, for the second year in succession, a Clark Gable film won the Best Picture Oscar.

Following Harlow's death in 1937 Gable's regular partners became Spencer Tracy and Myrna Loy, and, off screen, there was the famous marriage to actress Carole Lombard (see pages 17–18). He appeared with Tracy in the spectacular *San Francisco* (1936), featuring a memorable earthquake, but the teaming with Loy the following year produced less satisfactory results. *Parnell* (1937), the story of the 19th-century Irish politician, was one of Gable's few disasters. It failed at the box office and was panned by the critics. He bounced back assuredly with two fine actioners co-starring Tracy, *Test Pilot* (1938) and *Boom Town* (1940), the former also featuring Loy.

■ ■ ■
ABOVE
Gable's Oscar-winning performance in *It Happened One Night* (1934). Claudette Colbert is about to prove that the leg is mightier than the thumb when it comes to hitching a ride.
■ ■ ■

CLARK GABLE

Sandwiched in between was his greatest role, the one from which he is inseparable; Rhett Butler in *Gone With the Wind* (1939). While the search for Scarlett O'Hara reached epic proportions, there was only ever one Rhett Butler. Arrogant, strong, humorous, sexual, charming, vigorous, rugged and independent – Gable had all the necessary qualities in abundance. Another Oscar nomination followed, but he was the film's only major nominee to lose out, beaten by a showier performance from Robert Donat as Mr Chips.

In 1942 Gable, still distraught after the death of Carole Lombard, signed up for war service in the USAF. He reached the rank of major and received medals for his part in the bombing raids over Germany. After his discharge he immediately returned to films with *Adventure* (1945), featuring MGM's latest female star, Greer Garson. 'Gable's back and Garson's got him!' screamed the posters, but the film was poor and Gable disliked both the picture and his co-star. And, although he remained a star until his death in 1960, he was never to regain the quality films and roles he had been offered before the war – not even in the remake of *Red Dust*, *Mogambo* (1953). His personal life was little better, until he met and married his fifth wife, Kay Spreckels, with whom he happily remained until his death.

His one truly classic post-war movie is the aforementioned *The Misfits* in which Gable plays an ageing cowboy, a man out of time, trying to etch out a living rounding up the rapidly diminishing wild horses in Reno. It was a great performance, but a tragic movie. Not only did it prove to be both Gable's and Monroe's final movie, it also greatly contributed to Gable's death. He insisted on doing many of his own stunts (partly in an attempt to pass the time while waiting for Monroe to appear in front of the cameras) and died of a heart attack, on 16 November 1960, shortly after completing the film. Even more tragically, he died a few months before the birth of his only child.

'Gable has enemies all right, but they all like him.' – producer David O Selznick.

Manhattan Melodrama (1934), starred Gable and William Powell as two boys growing up in the New York slums, one to become a gangster and the other district attorney. This routine, enjoyable MGM movie gained a certain notoriety when public enemy number one John Dillinger was shot by G-men outside the cinema after having watched the movie.

In new screen splendor...
The most magnificent picture ever!

DAVID O. SELZNICK'S PRODUCTION OF MARGARET MITCHELL'S

"GONE WITH THE WIND"

STARRING

CLARK GABLE
VIVIEN LEIGH
LESLIE HOWARD OLIVIA de HAVILLAND

A SELZNICK INTERNATIONAL PICTURE · VICTOR FLEMING · SCREEN PLAY BY SIDNEY HOWARD · METRO-GOLDWYN-MAYER INC · Music by MAX STEINER

TEEN STARS AND BEEFCAKE

The '50s and '60s were the great decades for the teen stars and beefcakes. They were constantly featured in a series of Italian sword and sandal movies, Tarzan films, juvenile delinquent rock 'n' roll flicks, westerns and low-budget science fiction movies; not to mention the never-ending stream of fan magazines, keeping the moviegoers informed of the latest gossip and entertained with plentiful glossy pin-ups.

JEFF CHANDLER
1918 ★ 1961

Jeff Chandler falls firmly into the beefcake camp, always looking too old to be a teen star due to his prematurely greying hair. He came to notice playing Indians, notably Cochise in the pro-Indian western *Broken Arrow* (1950), for which Chandler won an Oscar nomination as Best Supporting Actor. Throughout the first half of the '50s Chandler stuck with the western, starring in films with such great oater titles as *The Battle at Apache Pass* (1952; as Cochise again) and *The Great Sioux Uprising* (1953). He also reprised his Cochise role yet again, unbilled, in *Taza, Son of Cochise* (1954). As the '50s progressed, Chandler branched out into thrillers, *Female on the Beach* (1955) with Joan Crawford; war movies, *Away All Boats!* (1956); and melodramas, *Return to Peyton Place* (1961). At the time of his death, through blood poisoning following surgery for a slipped disc, his career showed no sign of wavering. If Chandler had lived longer it seems likely he would have become a major star of the small screen. He would have been ideal as the patriarch in a soap opera.

STEVE COCHRAN
1917 ★ 1965

In 1950 Steve Cochran seemed to have a bright future. He had played minor roles in 'Boston Blackie' and Danny Kaye movies, before landing a

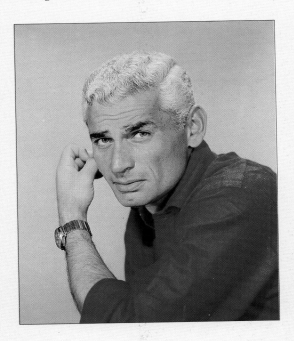

FAR LEFT
Jeff Chandler rose to fame playing Indians, but later proved himself adaptable to any genre.

LEFT
Steve Cochran never seemed to fulfil his potential despite playing the lead in an early film by leading Italian director Michelangelo Antonioni. Cochran is seen here in the 1949 gangster movie, *White Heat.*

notable part in the classic James Cagney gangster movie *White Heat* (1949) and the male lead in the Ku Klux Klan thriller *Storm Warning* (1950), also starring Doris Day and Ginger Rogers. This was to remain his best role. It is a much underrated movie and Cochran turns in a delightfully slimy performance. With the exception of *Come Next Spring* (1955) and Antonioni's *Il Grido* (1957; *The Cry*), his remaining '50s films were incredibly ordinary, and by the last years of the decade he was appearing in exploitation movies, like *I, Mobster* (1958) and *The Beat Generation* (1959; *This Rebel Age*). He died of acute lung infection on 15 June 1965.

NICK ADAMS
1931 ★ 1968

Nick Adams was a leading cinema juvenile delinquent, part of the fated cast of *Rebel Without a Cause* (1955). He was also successful on television, with the western series 'The Rebel' (1959–60) and as a newspaper reporter in 'Saints and Sinners' (1962). His big screen career continued to flourish

■ ■ ■
BELOW
Nick Adams starred in one of Boris Karloff's lesser horror movies, *Die Monster Die* (1965) which was based on a story by H P Lovecraft.
■ ■ ■

during the early '60s, with a supporting role in Don Siegel's war movie *Hell is for Heroes* (1962) and an Oscar nomination as Best Supporting Actor in *Twilight of Honor* (1963; *The Charge is Murder*). But lead roles only came from the world of low budget, exploitation film-making, and so Adams starred in *Young Dillinger* (1964), *Die, Monster, Die* (1965; *Monster of Terror*) and *Frankenstein Conquers the World* (1965; *Frankenstein versus the Giant Fish/Frankenstein and the Giant Lizard*). The energetic, low-budget horrors of the '60s provided more fun than many of Hollywood's more respectable, better-publicized productions, but were hardly Oscar material. He was found dead on 7 February 1968, the result of an overdose of drugs, which he had been taking for a nervous disorder.

JEFFREY HUNTER
1925 ★ 1969

Jeffrey Hunter was a better teen idol than actor, wisely having changed his name from Henry Herman McKinnies, which might have seemed just a little out of place in the teen magazines. This was not to say that Hunter was a bad actor or did not appear in good films. He was fine in John Wayne's classic western *The Searchers* (1956) as the half-caste Martin Pawley and was a popular star for over a decade. However, he was somewhat improbably cast in the lead role in the stolid *King of Kings* (1961) as Jesus, causing critics to dub the movie 'I Was a Teenage Jesus'. Even worse than the casting, the film lasted an unbelievable 161 minutes. As the '60s progressed Hunter fell out of favour, his main employment coming from obscure exploitation flicks. He was seen in the spy movie *Dimension 5* (1966), *A Witch Without a Broom* (1966) and the European sexploitation movie *Sexy Susan at the King's Court* (1968). A year later he was dead, the result of injuries sustained in a serious fall in his home which required brain surgery.

nude calendar shot. 'I was broke and needed the money', she admitted when the photograph was resurrected later in her career. There were also a few bit parts in minor films. The most frequently seen today is probably The Marx Brothers' *Love Happy* (1949), which she made after her contract with Fox had lapsed. She then met Johnny Hyde, an influential agent who soon became Monroe's lover. It was Hyde who arranged her audition for *The Asphalt Jungle* (1950), shortly before his death. *The Asphalt Jungle* is Monroe's first significant role. Although it was only a small part, she made quite an impression as Louis Calhern's mistress and followed it up with another important minor role, in *All About Eve* (1950). The film won her another contract with Fox.

She continued to gain more exposure and fans, mainly through her constant pin-up work. She did, however, continue to appear in films during this period. They were mostly forgettable, but she was finally given an important dramatic role in Fritz Lang's thriller *Clash by Night* (1952). Monroe was obviously on the crest of a gigantic wave, yet many colleagues from the period talk of her insecurity, a problem which would later plague her career.

For the time being everything seemed perfect. Her next role was opposite Cary Grant and Ginger Rogers in the Howard Hawks' comedy *Monkey Business* (1952). It is not a great film, but she was working with the top Hollywood talent and obviously in line for her first starring role. It came with the psychological thriller *Don't Bother to Knock* (1952), but the film was not a great success. According to the director Roy Ward Baker, 'She had done a lot of work previously but she was frightened to death and you had to drag a performance out of her line by line. But I was dealing with a very special personality that needed very special treatment, so I gave it to her.' Most critics felt she was tackling a role that was, at least at this stage in Monroe's career, beyond her.

Niagara (1952) presented no such problems; she was perfectly cast as the deadly seductress, wiggling across the screen and to certain stardom. The film was a huge hit, and she consolidated her success with two big budget, empty musicals, *Gentlemen Prefer Blondes* (1953) and *There's No Business Like Show Business* (1954), plus an equally vacuous comedy, *How to Marry a Millionaire* (1953). The first of these was undoubtedly the best, mainly due to the winning combination of Monroe and Jane Russell.

By now her reputation as difficult to work with began to grow, partly because of Monroe's over-reliance on her drama coach, Natasha Lytess. She often insisted on shooting simple scenes over and over again and arrived late on the set. She certainly irritated Otto Preminger, her director on *River of No Return* (1954), a good western in which she was well teamed with Robert Mitchum. The films stands

■ ■ ■

ABOVE
Niagara (1952), the film that clinched Monroe's success as the media concentrated on 'the Monroe wiggle'. 'A raging torrent of emotion that even nature can't control,' claimed the posters, but were they referring to Monroe or the famous waterfall?

■ ■ ■

BELOW
Otto Preminger was one of many directors frustrated at working with Monroe, but *River of No Return* (1954), with Robert Mitchum, was one of her more enjoyable pictures of the period.

■ ■ ■

■ ■ ■
ABOVE
The archetypal Monroe
image from *The Seven
Year Itch* (1955), her first
film with famed director
Billy Wilder. Tom Ewell
looks on admiringly.
■ ■ ■

■ ■ ■
RIGHT
Monroe's marriage to
baseball star Joe
DiMaggio in 1954 was
front page news; the
marriage lasted just nine
months.
■ ■ ■

up better than her bigger budget, better-known movies from this period. At this time press speculation was rife about her relationship with baseball star Joe DiMaggio and on 14 January 1954 they were married.

In 1954 Monroe also had a run-in with Fox, over the quality of her roles and her salary. She was now a big enough star to get what she wanted. And what she got was *The Seven Year Itch* (1955) with one of Hollywood's greatest directors, Billy Wilder. The play had already been a big hit and the film version was eagerly awaited. *The Seven Year Itch* contains perhaps the classic Monroe image, the famous skirt-blowing scene as she stands over a subway grating to be cooled by the draft of air. The filming of the scene, which naturally attracted many interested onlookers, as well as the press, angered DiMaggio. Less than a month later, and after less than nine months of marriage, their relationship came to an end.

However, no sooner were they divorced than rumours began spreading about a possible reunion, capped when they appeared together at the première of *The Seven Year Itch*. The film perfectly

displayed her talent for comedy and received excellent reviews. She was also attempting to grasp more control of her career, forming Marilyn Monroe Productions. The company's first film was *The Prince and the Showgirl* (1957) with Laurence Olivier.

Meanwhile Monroe was also intent on improving her craft, studying at the famed Actors Studio run by Lee Strasberg, as well as preparing to star in *Bus Stop* (1956). Monroe gave a fine performance in *Bus Stop*, and is ably supported by Don Murray. However, the story of a simple cowboy falling for a chanteuse and trying to forcibly take her back to his farm seems particularly misogynous when seen today, and makes uncomfortable viewing.

By this time Monroe was involved in the second famous relationship of her life, with respected playwright Arthur Miller, a pairing the press would dub 'The Hourglass and the Egghead'. They were married on 1 July 1956. Monroe was obviously in love with Miller. He provided her with, among other things, the security and respect she so desired. Unfortunately this security did not translate to the set of *The Prince and the Showgirl* where relations between Monroe and Olivier, who was also directing the picture, became strained. Nevertheless, the result on screen was enjoyable if not spectacular.

In 1957 Monroe announced she was pregnant. Tragically, on 1 August that year she suffered the first of her three miscarriages. Monroe found her

MARILYN MONROE WEDS DIMAGGIO

failure to bear children difficult to cope with, and donated her time to children's charities. Nevertheless, her film career was about to reach its peak when she began preparations for *Some Like It Hot* (1959), which reunited her with Billy Wilder. *Some Like It Hot* is the perfect Hollywood comedy; there's romance, good songs, likeable characters, a splendid supporting cast and, above all, humour in abundance. And, to top it all, Monroe is seen here at her most erotic. It is the film which best captures the screen persona of Monroe. The character of Sugar Kane is an equal mixture of sex, wit, innocence and vulnerability. Who could resist her when she claims 'I always get the fuzzy end of the lollipop'? Her mixture of innocence and sexuality is seen to best effect in the scene where she repeatedly kisses Tony Curtis, who feigns indifference.

Filming, however, was nowhere near as smooth as the end result suggests. She consistently appeared late on set and required numerous retakes, often unable to remember the simplest line. Supposedly 'It's me, Sugar' took Monroe 37 takes to get right. Jewish co-star Tony Curtis made the remark, 'Kissing her is like kissing Hitler'. Wilder was no more complimentary: 'She has breasts like granite and a brain like Swiss cheese, full of holes. Extracting a performance from her is like pulling teeth.' To cap it all, she was pregnant again, and for the second time she lost her child.

Monroe's next film was *Let's Make Love* (1960), co-starring Yves Montand. An inconsequential picture, it is recalled now as much for her affair with Montand as the results on screen. It was not to be a lasting relationship and she was soon involved in the production of *The Misfits* (1961), which Miller had written specially for her. It is therefore not surprising that her character should seem the closest she got to playing herself. She was also working with an excellent cast – Clark Gable, Montgomery Clift, Eli Wallach, Thelma Ritter –

and had, in John Huston, one of Hollywood's best directors. The result is a superb film (see pages 48 and 63), with Monroe giving an excellent performance. It was a fitting climax to her career.

The Misfits was another difficult film to make; Monroe's marriage to Miller was disintegrating, she was becoming increasingly reliant on pills and alcohol and was, yet again, frequently late on set. Shortly after filming was completed Monroe sunk to her lowest point when she was admitted to the Payne Whitney Psychiatric Clinic by her psychiatrist. She turned to DiMaggio, again fuelling press speculation about a possible reconciliation.

■ ■ ■
BELOW
Bus Stop (1956) brought Monroe good reviews. The film featured in both the *New York Times* and The National Board of Review's ten best movies of 1956.
■ ■ ■

Once again Monroe bounced back, and seemed
to recover so well that work began on another film,
the prophetically titled *Something's Got to Give*. Yet
again, she frequently failed to appear on set and
was fired from the picture. She died on 5 August
1962 from a barbiturates overdose, which the
coroner claimed was a 'probable suicide'. Many
close to her strenuously deny that Monroe would
have committed suicide. Further speculation
surrounds her death through her involvement with
both John and Robert Kennedy. Robert Kennedy
was said to have visited her just hours before her
death. This has led to a number of conspiracy
theories, particularly that Monroe was murdered by
the FBI or CIA in an attempt to discredit the
Kennedys. Whatever the truth might be, Hollywood
had lost a fine comedienne, a good dramatic actress
and possibly its greatest star.

Not surprisingly Hollywood has not let such a
hot property rest. Shortly after her death there was a
documentary narrated by Rock Hudson called
Marilyn (1963). Films inspired by her life were also
popular. The first, *The Goddess* (1958), appeared
four years before her death. There have since been
a number of sexploitation films, three TV movies –
The Sex Symbol (1974), *This Year's Blonde* (1980)
and *Marilyn: The Untold Story* (1980) – and Larry
Buchanan's exploitation flick *Goodbye Norma Jean*
(1976). It is highly likely the Monroe industry will
continue rolling for many years to come.

*Marilyn Monroe was famed for her quotes, such
as:*
*'Sex is a part of nature and I go along with
nature.'*

*'They spend a lot of time worrying about
whether a girl has a cleavage or not. It seems to
me they ought to worry if she doesn't have any.'*
*'A sex symbol becomes a thing. I hate being a
thing.'*

*Q: 'Did you have anything on when you posed
for that calendar?'*
A: 'Yes. The radio.'

Q: 'What do you wear in bed?'
A: 'Chanel No. 5.'

Q: 'What made you study acting?'
A: 'Seeing my own pictures.'

Q: 'Is it true you wear falsies?'
A: 'Those who know me better know better.'

*Monroe's directors had the following comments
to make:*
*'Directing her was like directing Lassie. You
needed 14 takes to get each one of them right.' –
Otto Preminger.*

*'Anyone can remember lines, but it takes a real
artist to come on the set and not know her lines
and give the performance she did.' – Billy
Wilder.*

*'As near genius as any actress I ever knew.' –
Joshua Logan.*

Los Angeles Times MONDAY FINAL

Times Telephone Numbers:
MAdison 8-4411—Classified Advertising
MAdison 8-2345—For all other calls.
Circulation—Largest in the West:
772,439 Daily; 1,196,183 Sunday.

LIBERTY UNDER THE LAW   TRUE INDUSTRIAL FREEDOM

VOL. LXXXI   SIX PARTS—PART ONE   MONDAY MORNING, AUGUST 6, 1962   KTTV (Channel 11)   92 PAGES   DAILY 10c

MARILYN MONROE FOUND DEAD
Sleeping Pill Overdose Blamed

1913 ★ 1964

A L A N   L A D D

Pint-size Alan Ladd played bit parts in scores of films throughout the 1930s and early '40s. He had been in Laurel and Hardy movies, horror flicks like *The Black Cat* (1941) and crime fighting serials such as *The Green Hornet* (1940). He even turned up in *Citizen Kane* (1941). Ladd must have thought fame and fortune had passed him by when he landed the role of the ruthless killer in *This Gun for Hire* (1942), based on Graham Greene's novel *A Gun for Sale*. Not only did it bring him to prominence with film audiences, it also marked the beginning of a productive four-film partnership with Veronica Lake. So entwined did the two become in the public eye, they also had guest roles in two other movies.

Their first appearance together was certainly their best. *This Gun for Hire* is still a fine, surprisingly downbeat, thriller. The film established Ladd's image: cool, tough, gun in hand, trenchcoat with upturned collar, and expressionless, rarely smiling, face. It was an image that would serve him well for 20 years. It was to be a good year for Ladd. He also married his agent, Sue Carol, and was teamed for a second time with Veronica Lake in a remake of Dashiell Hammett's *The Glass Key* (1942). This was another first-rate crime movie, with Ladd cast in a slightly more heroic role. However, his thunder was rather stolen by William Bendix, who turned in a wonderfully vicious performance in a supporting role. Fans had to wait another four years before the next Ladd-Lake pairing, this time in *The Blue Dahlia* (1946). Another thriller (a soldier returning from the war finds himself suspected of his wife's murder), this time from a script by ace crime novelist Raymond Chandler. It was again a well above average feature. However, their next film,

Saigon (1947), had routine written all over it, with no respected author to provide a solid base as in their other three offerings. It was to be their final film together.

The rest of Ladd's career is almost entirely composed of routine movies: ordinary thrillers, ordinary westerns and ordinary war films. *The Great Gatsby* (1949) is notable as much for its famous source, F Scott Fitzgerald's novel, as the results on screen. And *The Black Knight* (1954) is remembered for its bizarre casting of Ladd in a tale of when knights were bold, as strange as Tony Curtis and his Bronx accent in the similar *The Black Shield of Falworth* (1954). The film was partly redeemed by a typically excellent British supporting cast which featured Peter Cushing and André Morell.

Towering above anything else in Ladd's filmography, aside from the aforementioned films

■ ■ ■

ABOVE
Alan Ladd's perfect partner was Veronica Lake. They are seen together in their first and best pairing, *This Gun for Hire* (1942).

■ ■ ■

played by Jack Palance. As with most classic Hollywood movies, there is a great supporting cast, from the young Brandon de Wilde who idolizes Shane to the perennial victim Elisha Cook Jnr, ruthlessly murdered on the town's muddy streets by Palance. The film was directed with meticulous care by George Stevens. Perhaps too much care, giving the film a slightly self-conscious, calculated air. But it still remains a marvellous achievement.

Nothing later even remotely equalled *Shane*. It would have been interesting to have seen Ladd in the role of Jett Rink in Stevens' *Giant* (1956), but he turned it down, believing himself too old for the part. He would probably have made a better job than James Dean, who was finally cast. His last film, released in 1964, was the big budget, enjoyably trashy, overblown melodrama *The Carpetbaggers* (1964). However, by the time it appeared on the cinema screens Ladd was dead through a lethal dose of alcohol and pills taken on 29 January 1964. It has been suggested he committed suicide, just as his mother had done 27 years earlier by drinking ant poison. However, the coroner told Ladd's son David that there was neither enough alcohol nor sleeping pills in Ladd's system to call it suicide. 'It was just that magic number,' he said, 'that magic combination – whatever it is – that you just don't wake up from.'

'Most popular actors dislike being seen in public, but Alan was unusually averse to it. I once helped Sue Ladd convince her husband to accept an invitation to a Royal Command Performance in London. After he finally agreed, he said to me, "They'll all see how short I am."' – Screenwriter Richard Maibaum in Close Ups: The Move Star Book, *edited by Danny Peary.*

'Alan Ladd is hard, bitter and occasionally charming, but he is, after all, a small boy's idea of a tough guy.' – Raymond Chandler.

■ ■ ■
TOP
Alan Ladd was improbably cast in the title role in *The Black Knight* (1954).
■ ■ ■

ABOVE
Unarguably Ladd's best role, as the gunfighter *Shane* (1953), which re-established him as one of the top ten box office attractions.
■ ■ ■

with Lake, is the classic western *Shane* (1953). If someone has only seen one Alan Ladd film, chances are that it is *Shane*. He plays the archetypal stranger with a mysterious background, who comes to town and protects the powerless homesteaders against the evil hired gun, brilliantly

Hollywood. In 1958 he was teamed with Marlon Brando and Dean Martin in the war epic *The Young Lions* (1958) for director Edward Dmytryk, while the following year he made *Suddenly Last Summer* (1959) with director Joseph L Mankiewicz, Katharine Hepburn and Elizabeth Taylor. This version of the Tennessee Williams' play gained instant notoriety, featuring such late '50s taboo-breaking topics as homosexuality, rape and cannibalism. It prompted leading British critic C A Lejeune to comment: 'I loathe this film, I say so candidly. To my mind it is a decadent piece of work, sensational, barbarous and ridiculous.' On a personal level, Clift's drinking was becoming more of a problem. He often arrived on the set late and unprepared, provoking the displeasure of his directors and fellow actors.

The 1960s opened with his most underrated movie, *Wild River* (1960), on which he finally worked with Elia Kazan. In essence it is an American version of *The Last Days of Dolwyn* (1949), as Clift tries to convince an old woman to leave the valley where she lives before it is flooded, but it has far more emotional power than the British movie. Next came his last great movie, *The Misfits* (1961), directed by John Huston. The film's haunting beauty and aura of melancholy is increased by the final appearance of two Hollywood greats, Marilyn Monroe and Clark Gable, and the knowledge that Montgomery Clift was also only five years from his death. However, he did gain another Oscar nomination, this time as Best Supporting Actor, for his performance in the self-important *Judgment at Nuremberg* (1962), which told of the Nazi war criminal trials, and was reunited with John Huston for the overlong, partially successful biopic *Freud* (1963).

Freud had a particularly troubled production, hardly helped by Clift's fear that he was going blind. Immediately after filming was completed he had an operation for cataracts on both eyes. Work

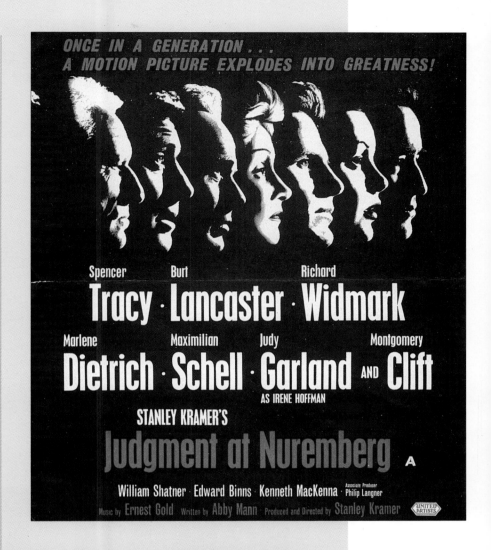

was now becoming increasingly scarce for Clift. His friend Elizabeth Taylor did secure him a part in her latest picture, *Reflections in a Golden Eye* (1967), but he died of a heart attack on 23 July 1966, two months before filming began.

'Liz is the only woman I have ever met who turns me on. She feels like the other half of me.' – Montgomery Clift.

'I'm trying to be an actor. Not a movie star, just an actor.' – Montgomery Clift.

ABOVE
Clift won an Oscar nomination as Best Supporting Actor for his performance in the all-star *Judgment at Nuremberg* (1962). He agreed to play the part for nothing after his agent had demanded a large fee for the actor. He sent the agent his commission: a large paper bag containing nothing.

1913 ★ 1967

VIVIEN LEIGH

If Vivien Leigh had retired from films in 1939,
only four years after making her movie debut, she
would have been assured a lasting place in the film
history books for her performance as Scarlett
O'Hara in *Gone With the Wind* (1939). The
legendary search for Scarlett O'Hara, when
producer David O Selznick tested hundreds of
actresses for the leading role, is almost as famous
as the film itself. In fact, the search was turned into
a TV movie, *The Scarlett O'Hara War* (1980).

The very British Leigh was born in Darjeeling,
India, and only came to England when she was
seven. She enrolled at RADA in 1932, made her
stage debut in 1934 and had a hit the following year
with *The Green Sash* at the Q Theatre in London.
Her movie debut was not far behind; a supporting
role in the Ciceley Courtneidge–Max Miller
comedy *Things Are Looking Up* (1935). A rather
prophetic title. Two years later she was starring

with future husband Laurence Olivier in the Spanish Armada drama *Fire Over England* (1937) and with Conrad Veidt in another period drama, *Dark Journey* (1937). The next year, 1938, proved even better, appearing opposite Rex Harrison, and being overshadowed by Charles Laughton, in *St Martin's Lane* (1938; *Sidewalks of London*). More significant was *A Yank at Oxford* (1938), with an over-age Robert Taylor playing the title role and falling for Maureen O'Sullivan. Leigh was cast in the role of the town flirt in this popular MGM production and it was instrumental in her being cast as Scarlett.

And so to *Gone With the Wind*. Whole books have been devoted to this film and it is still shown in cinemas, most recently to coincide with its 50th birthday celebrations. Such a legend has grown around the film that objective criticism can be difficult. It is undoubtedly a fine epic melodrama, with a superb cast, unbeatable production values, some excellent performances and an unforgettable score. But it is not faultless. Leslie Howard, in a role he detested, irritates and, at times, it is difficult to care about the characters. But on a large screen, in a packed cinema, it remains an experience to be savoured. And Leigh is perfect as the flirtatious, scheming Scarlett O'Hara, delivering one of the cinema's most famous final lines – 'After all, tomorrow is another day'. The role won her that year's Oscar as Best Actress.

In 1940 she divorced her first husband and married Laurence Olivier, with whom she had been romantically involved since 1936. Their marriage is almost as famous as Leigh's films and lasted, at times rather turbulently, until 1961. They immediately appeared together in *That Hamilton Woman* (1941; *Lady Hamilton*) for Alexander Korda. This turgid tale of Horatio Nelson and Emma Hamilton was reputedly Winston Churchill's favourite film, but it was a surprisingly passionless affair. Their projected teaming in Hitchcock's

Rebecca (1940), before Leigh's success as Scarlett made her unsuitable for mousy roles, would have been more interesting. Much better was her reteaming with Robert Taylor, the previous year, in *Waterloo Bridge* (1940), which provided Leigh with one of her finest roles. She plays Myra, a ballet dancer, who falls in love with a soldier during World War I and, through a series of misunderstandings, sinks into prostitution. Wartime London was atmospherically recreated in the MGM studios by director Mervyn LeRoy.

The remainder of the '40s was something of an anti-climax. In the cinema she starred in George Bernard Shaw's *Caesar and Cleopatra* (1945), at the time Britain's most expensive movie and a flop, and yet another version, albeit a well-staged one, of *Anna Karenina* (1947). She was upstaged in the later movie by the superb Ralph Richardson. Away from the screen, she had made her American stage debut in 1941 in *Romeo and Juliet* and had also toured the Middle East for three months in 1943 entertaining troops.

■ ■ ■
ABOVE LEFT
Despite leading French director Julien Duvivier and support from the excellent Ralph Richardson, *Anna Karenina* (1947) failed to match Garbo's '30s version.
■ ■ ■

■ ■ ■

ABOVE
Leigh's last film was
Ship of Fools (1965); her
role was cut to little
more than a cameo.

■ ■ ■

■ ■ ■

RIGHT
Karl Malden confronts
Leigh in her last great
success, *A Streetcar
Named Desire* (1951),
which saw her named
Best Actress at the
Venice Film Festival and
by the New York Film
Critics, and won her the
year's Oscar and BAFTA.

■ ■ ■

Vivien Leigh also contracted tuberculosis in 1945, causing her to withdraw from the play *Skin of Our Teeth*, and she spent nine months convalescing at Notley Abbey. Prior to this she had suffered a miscarriage, brought on by an accident on the set of *Caesar and Cleopatra*. The resulting period of depression halted production. It is these periods of illness throughout her life that partly accounts for the relatively few films she made.

The '50s started in brighter fashion. Leigh repeated her stage role as Blanche Dubois in Elia Kazan's highly acclaimed version of Tennessee Williams' *A Streetcar Named Desire* (1951), in which she played opposite the young and electrifying Marlon Brando. She was Williams' own choice for the role and won her her second Oscar. But good movies became increasingly scarce for Leigh as she suffered a series of mental breakdowns and periods of depression. A nervous breakdown during the production of *Elephant Walk* (1954) forced her to leave the production. Elizabeth Taylor took over the role, although Leigh can still be seen in some long shots taken on location in Ceylon (now

Sri Lanka). She did have an unsuccessful second stab at Tennessee Williams with *The Roman Spring of Mrs Stone* (1961), after having turned down *Suddenly Last Summer* (1959), since she had no wish to play a middle-aged mother.

Her final film was the all-star melodrama *Ship of Fools* (1965). Unfortunately, her role was much cut and Lee Marvin was added to the list of co-stars with whom she reputedly did not get along, a list which also includes Clark Gable and Marlon Brando, co-stars in her greatest successes. But these successes were far behind her and by 1967 she was dead, a result of her tuberculosis, at 54.

'She made life hell for everybody near her, unless they did everything she wished, as she wished and when she wished.' – Wolfe Kaufman obviously not too enamoured with Vivien Leigh.

'My birth sign is Scorpio and they eat themselves up and burn themselves out. I swing between happiness and misery. I am part prude and part non-conformist. I say what I think and I don't pretend and I am prepared to accept the consequences of my actions.' – Vivien Leigh in Vivien: The Life of Vivien Leigh, *by Alexander Walker.*

1922 ★ 1969

JUDY GARLAND

Judy Garland's career almost encapsulates 20th-century entertainment. She made her debut in vaudeville, supposedly at the age of 2½, was popular on the radio in the '30s, was one of the movies' biggest stars of the '40s, found equal success with her recording career and concerts of the '50s, before making a series of television specials in the '60s. All this wrapped in the worst clichés of showbiz life; failed marriages, nervous breakdowns, suicide attempts, drug problems et al.

She appeared on the stage as a child under her real name, Frances Gumm, as part of The Gumm Sisters, who reputedly changed their names after having it misspelled as The Glumm Sisters on a theatre marquee. By the time she was 12 Garland was signed with MGM, the studio which produced many classic musicals during the '40s and '50s. Before making any movies, however, she became a hit on the radio through regular appearances on the Bob Hope Show.

Her movie debut came at the age of 14 in *Every Sunday* (1936), a short which co-starred her with Deanna Durbin. More films followed, most notably *Love Finds Andy Hardy* (1938), the first of her three appearances in MGM's popular Andy Hardy series and the start of a successful partnership with fellow child star Mickey Rooney. Their best movie together is probably *Babes in Arms* (1939), directed by master choreographer Busby Berkeley. The film is an archetypal putting-on-a-show musical, but its strength is in the playing by the leads and some first-rate songs, three of which later turned up in *Singin' in the Rain* (1952).

But the film which sealed Garland's star status was *The Wizard of Oz* (1939). It provided her with her most famous part as Dorothy – a role that had

initially been intended for Shirley Temple. The film, which is constantly revived on television, is almost perfection; the performances of Ray Bolger (The Scarecrow), Jack Haley (The Tin Man), Bert Lahr (The Cowardly Lion), Frank Morgan (The Wizard) and Margaret Hamilton (The Wicked

■ ■ ■

LEFT
Judy Garland's first regular partner was the young Mickey Rooney, a big box office attraction following his success in the Andy Hardy films. They made seven films together between 1938 and 1943.

■ ■ ■

BELOW LEFT
The ever wonderful *The Wizard of Oz* (1939) featuring Dorothy (Garland), The Scarecrow (Ray Bolger), The Tin Man (Jack Haley), The Wizard (Frank Morgan) and The Cowardly Lion (Bert Lahr).

■ ■ ■

■ ■ ■

ABOVE
Garland's best role,
alongside Dorothy,
came in Vincente
Minnelli's magnificent
Meet Me in St Louis
(1944).

■ ■ ■

BELOW
Judy Garland and Gene
Kelly's best film
together, *The Pirate*
(1948), was one of four
films Vincente Minnelli
directed featuring
Garland.

■ ■ ■

The Harvey Girls (1946), featuring the excellent number 'On the Atchison, Topeka and the Santa Fé', a fine musical with Fred Astaire, *Easter Parade* (1948), and a rare dramatic success with *The Clock* (1945; *Under the Clock*; see pages 28–29).

Many of these films were directed by her husband Vincente Minnelli and produced by Arthur Freed, as was the best, the magnificent *Meet Me in St Louis* (1944). This is the perfect family melodrama, wrapped up in excellent turn-of-the-century period detail, with fine ensemble playing from the perfect cast and, the icing on the cake, a collection of superb songs. It is impossible to pick one highlight from a score featuring 'The Boy Next Door', 'The Trolley Song', 'Have Yourself a Merry Little Christmas', and 'Meet Me in St Louis'. The film avoids cloying sentimentality by the amazing performance from Margaret O'Brien as Garland's younger sister Tootie, with the memorable Hallowe'en sequence and the quite chilling destruction of her snowman which she cannot take on the family's move to New York. The darker side of childhood is the unexpected pleasure provided by *Meet Me in St Louis*.

By the '50s, however, Garland's film career was in tatters, not least due to her own unreliability. There were the problems on *Summer Stock*, she was suspended by MGM during the production of *Annie Get Your Gun* (1950), which the studio had purchased for her and she lost a part opposite Fred Astaire in *Royal Wedding* (1951; *Wedding Bells*) through ill health. None of the other studios were interested in working with Garland after she had been dropped by MGM. To make matters worse her marriage to Minnelli was also breaking up. The exhausted Garland made her first suicide attempt, trying to cut her throat with broken glass.

Her luck had actually begun to turn by 1952 when she married her personal manager Sid Luft. It was Luft who arranged Garland's European concert

Witch of the West), not forgetting Toto the dog, could not have been bettered. The songs were equally memorable, with 'Over the Rainbow' the obvious standout and the song which would remain Garland's signature tune for the rest of her life. Surprisingly, the song was almost cut from the final version, MGM having decided that it slowed down the film. It was only reinstated through the persistence of producer Arthur Freed and songwriters Harold Arlen and E Y Harburg. Judy Garland's contribution to the movie earned her a richly deserved special Oscar 'for her outstanding performance as a screen juvenile'.

The '40s were full of excellent movies for Garland. She co-starred with Gene Kelly in his movie debut, *For Me and My Gal* (1942), which provided her with a more adult role. They went on to star in *The Pirate* (1948), their best movie together, and *Summer Stock* (1950; *If You Feel Like Singing*), an enjoyable musical with a troubled production due to Garland's frequent failure to turn up for filming. After completing the movie, producer Joe Pasternak decided to add another number, 'Get Happy', and recalled a now considerably slimmer Garland to shoot the sequence. The difference is quite apparent. The decade also produced

tour and her successful London Palladium shows. She was an even bigger hit on her return to the States, with her record 19-week engagement at New York's Palace Theatre. Garland finally appeared to be back at the top after completing her comeback film, *A Star is Born* (1954), for which she was nominated for an Oscar. But it was not to be. The film, which was considered too long by Warner Brothers, was cut by 27 minutes before general release, against the wishes of both Garland and director George Cukor. It damaged the picture and is also considered instrumental in Garland losing out on the Oscar she certainly deserved. *A Star is Born* was her last film for seven years.

Her life continued on a downward spiral, although there were plenty of shows, as well as her television specials during the '60s. There was even another Oscar nomination, as Best Supporting Actress for her performance in *Judgement at Nuremburg* (1961). But Garland was becoming increasingly dependent on alcohol and pills. In fact she had been taking the pills since her early days at MGM, where they had been prescribed by the studio doctor to help her cope with the gruelling schedule and in order to keep her weight down. Her marriage to Luft also failed and was followed by two further marriages, to Mark Heron and Mickey Deans, in the '60s. By the time she died in London on 22 June 1969 from an accidental overdose of sleeping pills, Garland was worn out. She was only 47, but photographs from her final years reveal a much older woman.

'Lana [Turner] was the beauty of the class [the school on the MGM lot for child performers] . . . In those days I was getting fatter and fatter – Lana just kept getting more beautiful. I used to gaze at her, and then become extremely conscious of the three candy bars I had eaten that morning!' – Judy Garland in 1948's Film Parade *annual.*

- - -

ABOVE
Judy Garland on the set of *Till the Clouds Roll By* (1945) with husband Vincente Minnelli, who directed her musical numbers in this movie. Garland was pregnant with Liza during filming.

- - -

LEFT
The *Daily News* reports Judy Garland's death in 1969 at the age of 47.

- - -

FAMOUS HOLLYWOOD MURDERS

The most infamous of all Hollywood murders must
be that of Sharon Tate (1943–1969), wife of director
Roman Polanski, who along with four others was
butchered by Charles Manson's gang in August
1969. Tate was actually little more than a starlet, a
glamorous actress who appeared in small, often
purely decorative roles. There were horror films,
Eye of the Devil and Polanski's *Dance of the
Vampires* (1967; *The Fearless Vampire Killers, or
Pardon Me, Your Teeth Are in My Neck*);
sensationalist melodramas, *Valley of the Dolls*
(1967); and spy spoofs, *The Wrecking Crew* (1969);
but the name of Tate is remembered today chiefly in
association with Manson. It is not so much her
being murdered that has kept Tate's name fresh in
the memory, but more the nature of the murders.
She was also eight months pregnant at the time.

On 8 August 1969 Tex Watson, Katie and Sadie
Mae Glutz, and Linda Kasabian, all members of

Manson's Family, cut the phone wires to Tate's
home at 10050 Cielo Drive in Hollywood. The first
person to die was 18-year-old Steven Parent, who
was shot by Watson in his car on the drive. On
entering the house, the gang rounded up Sharon
Tate and her three guests and demanded their
money. They not surprisingly quickly complied.
The gang then shot Jay Sebring, a 35-year-old
Hollywood hairdresser, while 32-year-old
Wojiciech Frykowski, a financier of an early
Polanski film, was repeatedly stabbed with a
doubled-edged knife by Sadie Mae Glutz, before
being shot twice and beaten about the head by
Watson. Watson then stabbed the wounded Sebring
and helped Katie Glutz to stab Abigail Folger in the
neck. Frykowski was amazingly still alive and
managed to reach the front door, before again being
repeatedly stabbed by Watson. The carnage

Manson and 3 girls guilty in slaying of Sharon Tate

CHICAGO DAILY NEWS

The Complete Home Newspaper

Cultists also convicted of 6 other murders

continued. Tate was held down while Watson killed her with the knife. Following this she was stabbed by the whole gang, who used her blood to daub the word 'pig' on the wall. The murders were over, leaving in their wake the bodies of Folger, Parent, Sebring, Tate and Frykowski. The following night two further murders were committed, this time the victims were Leno and Rosemary La Bianca, again in their own home.

The trial of Manson and the other members of 'The Family', which opened on 15 June 1970, was almost as famous as the murders. At nine and a half months it was America's longest murder trial and, naturally, front page news. Manson appeared in court with a cross on his forehead, which he had gouged on himself with a hacksaw blade. Other members of The Family followed his lead, as they later did when he shaved off his hair. President Nixon also involved himself in the trial, foolishly claiming Manson was guilty before the trial ended. On 29 March 1971 the four on trial were finally sentenced to death, which under California law meant life imprisonment.

The true horror of these murders is difficult to convey. Perhaps most disturbing, though, is the cult that has grown around Manson over the past 20 years, to the point where he is now almost a mini-industry. There have been numerous exploitation movies, books, fanzines, tee-shirts and records, many irresponsibly glamorizing him into simply an

anti-establishment cult figure. The fact that Manson was behind such horrific actions is conveniently glossed over.

Other Hollywood murders, thankfully, pale in comparison. The most famous case of the '20s was director William Desmond Taylor (see pages 9–10), while in the '30s there was the death of Thelma Todd (1905–35), an actress sometimes referred to as the 'Ice Cream Blonde'. She was found behind the wheel of her Lincoln Phaeton convertible in her garage, the victim of carbon monoxide poisoning. The official verdict was accidental death, although a cover-up has been suspected, fuelled by her husband's connections with organized crime, and New York gangsters such as Lucky Luciano.

The '40s brought another famous case, the 'Black Dahlia' murder. Black Dahlia was the nickname of Elizabeth Scott (1924–1947), an aspiring starlet. The case has lingered in the public memory because of the glamorous location, its brutal nature and the absence of a solution. On 15 January 1947 her body was found on waste ground in Los Angeles, beaten, bruised and cut in half at the waist, with the initials BD carved on her thigh. The murder brought a number of false confessions, that of Robert Manley attracting most attention. The case still remains open, has had several books written about it and inspired the film *True Confessions* (1981), starring Robert de Niro and Robert Duvall.

MYSTERY OVER FILM STAR'S DEATH DEEPENS
Murder, Suicide, Mishap? Police Cannot Decide

OTHER STARS 1960–1969

Dick Powell (1904–1963)

Dick Powell's career was remarkable for both its longevity and adaptability. He started as a crooner in Warner Brothers' musicals such as 42nd Street

(1933), Gold Diggers of 1933 *(1933) and* Footlight Parade *(1933). By the end of the decade their appeal, and Powell's, was on the wane. Then Powell had the fortune to star in a couple of good comedies, Preston Sturges'* Christmas in July *(1940) and René Clair's* It Happened Tomorrow *(1944), before landing the leading role of Philip Marlowe in* Farewell My Lovely *(1944;* Murder My Sweet*). This movie changed Powell's image from wet crooner to tough hero, a persona that was to last him until the early '50s. Once these roles dried up, he turned to directing and television production. He died from cancer on 2 January 1963.*

Jack Carson (1910–1963)

One of the cinema's most popular character stars and comic supporting actors was Canadian-born Jack Carson. He enlivened many a movie after making his debut in Stage Door *(1937). Following this drama, he appeared in Fritz Lang's gangster movie* You Only Live Once *(1937) and the comedy* Stand In *(1937), proving he was at home with any genre. Carson was later memorable in* A Star is Born *(1954) and* Cat on a Hot Tin Roof *(1958), but one of his most likeable roles was in the Doris Day musical*

It's a Great Feeling *(1949). The whole film centres around the fact that no-one wants to direct a film starring Jack Carson. He was much missed when he died from cancer on 2 January 1963.*

Zachary Scott (1914–1965)

Zachary Scott's best films all came in his first two years as a movie actor. He made his debut, appearing alongside Peter Lorre and Sydney Greenstreet, in The Mask of Dimitrios *(1944), a first-rate dark and moody thriller. This was followed the next year by his best role in* The Southerner *(1945), Jean Renoir's superb tale of hardship among poor farmers. The same year he also appeared in one of Joan Crawford's finest movies,* Mildred Pierce *(1945). Unfortunately, the remainder of his films were strictly routine, from* The Unfaithful *(1947), a rehash of* The Letter, *through the tired Glenn Ford movie* Appointment in Honduras *(1953) to the Jerry Lewis comedy* It's Only Money *(1962). He died from a brain tumour on 3 October 1965.*

Jayne Mansfield (1933–1967)

Jayne Mansfield epitomized the excesses of Hollywood and '50s sexuality, with her well-publicized 41-inch (104-centimetre) breasts, her home The Pink Palace, champagne fountains, her heart-shaped swimming pool and her obsession with pink. She is chiefly remembered for two films, the rock 'n' roll comedy The Girl Can't Help It *(1956) and* Will Success Spoil Rock Hunter? *(1957; Oh! For a Man!). Equally important to her status as a trash icon were her private life, particularly her marriage to body builder Mickey Hargitay, and her many poor films, such as* Promises, Promises *(1963), in which she appeared nude. Mansfield was decapitated in a car crash on 28 June 1967.*

CHICAGO DAILY NEWS

Warm | An Independent Newspaper | Final Markets **RED STREAK**
92d Year, Number 152 72 Pages | Thursday, June 29, 1967 | 10 Cents Phone 321-2000 | Stocks Down

Attorney, Chauffeur Die

Crash Kills Jayne Mansfield

Robert Taylor (1911–1969)

Spangler Arlington Brugh not surprisingly changed his name to Robert Taylor, and became one of MGM's most popular stars from the mid-1930s to the mid-1950s. This 20-year period saw Taylor starring opposite Irene Dunne in the weepie Magnificent Obsession *(1935), with Greta Garbo in* Camille *(1936), in Frank Borzage's* Three Comrades *(1938), alongside Vivien Leigh in* Waterloo Bridge *(1940), as* Billy the Kid *(1941) and* Ivanhoe *(1952), and in the epic* Quo Vadis *(1951). His last really good film was the western* The Last Hunt *(1955). By 1968, however, he was reduced to such forgettable movies as* The Day the Hot Line Got Hot *(1968). Taylor died on 8 June 1969 from lung cancer.*

THE ROCK 'N' ROLL STARS

Nearly all the great '50s rock 'n' rollers made at least one appearance in the movies, even if only a cameo in a Sam Katzman B-movie. It was Sam Katzman who started the ball rolling by starring Bill Haley in *Rock Around the Clock* (1956) and a quick, even cheaper, follow-up, *Don't Knock the Rock* (1957). He repeated the formula with Chubby Checker in *Twist Around the Clock* (1961) and *Don't Knock the Twist* (1962).

ELVIS PRESLEY
1935 ★ 1977

Elvis Presley starred in many more movies, and far more bad ones, than any of his contemporaries. He had taken the charts by storm and Hollywood was quick to capitalize, giving him a prominent role in the western *The Reno Brothers*. They also allowed him four songs and decided to rename the film after one of them, *Love Me Tender* (1956). Two late '50s films, *Jailhouse Rock* (1957) and *King Creole* (1958), marked his premature peak. They feature some great songs and *King Creole* even had a top

Hollywood director in Michael Curtiz. Then Elvis went into the army. His music was the chief victim, but his films also became more and more bland. They only remain of note due to his continuing appeal and the presence of a few old Hollywood reliables, like Barbara Stanwyck, and the odd '60s cult figure, such as Ursula Andress. But Hollywood nevertheless churned them out, at a rate of two a year for almost 15 years. Once the feature films dried up, there were a couple of documentaries. Even Elvis's death failed to stop the flow: the documentary *This is Elvis* (1981) and John Carpenter's television movie *Elvis* (1980) followed shortly after his death. Interestingly, the actor playing Presley in the 1980 movie, Kurt Russell, can be seen with Elvis as a child in *It Happened at the World's Fair* (1962).

BOBBY DARIN
1936 ★ 1973

Elvis might have chalked up the most films, but he never received the same critical praise as Bobby Darin found. Darin had a number of rock 'n' roll hits, the best being 'Splish Splash', before he changed his image to all-round entertainer and scored a massive success with 'Mack the Knife'. With the change of image Darin moved into films. Not rock 'n' roll flicks, but serious, often big budget films. There were supporting roles in the John Cassavettes jazz drama *Too Late Blues* (1961), the gritty war movie *Hell is for Heroes* (1962), and *Pressure Point* (1962), a psychological character study with Sidney Poitier. His role in *Captain Newman MD* (1963), a comedy drama starring Tony Curtis and Gregory Peck, brought Darin an Oscar nomination as Best Supporting Actor. He also married '60s teen idol Sandra Dee. By the mid-1960s, however, their marriage was over and Darin's movie career had also seen its best days. By 1973 he was dead, following open heart surgery.

RICKY NELSON
1940 ★ 1985

Ricky Nelson had a long showbusiness history. He was the son of bandleader Ozzie Nelson who, with his wife Harriet, appeared in the outstandingly popular television series, 'The Adventures of Ozzie and Harriet', between 1952 and 1965. Ricky also appeared in some of the shows, as well as their film *Here Come the Nelsons* (1952). However, he really came to prominence on the big screen with *Rio Bravo* (1959), the John Wayne film in which he played a young gunslinger. Not exactly a great actor, he was a perfect clean-cut teen idol. He had a lead role in *The Wackiest Ship in the Army* (1960), a Jack Lemmon comedy, but wisely concentrated more on his music than films during the remainder of his life. He died in a plane crash in 1985.

FIANCEE AND BAND AMONG VICTIMS IN SINGER'S PLANE AS EMERGENCY LANDING GOES WRONG

Rock star Nelson dies in jinx crash

EDDIE COCHRAN
1929 ★ 1960
AND
GENE VINCENT
1935 ★ 1971

Two of the '50s greatest rock 'n' rollers were Eddie
Cochran and Gene Vincent. They both appeared in
cameo roles in the classic rock 'n' roll comedy *The
Girl Can't Help It* (1956) and were travelling in the
same car, on a joint British tour in 1960, when it
crashed. It took Cochran's life and left Vincent
badly injured. Cochran had appeared in a couple of
'50s B teenflicks, *Untamed Youth* (1957), starring
'50s icon Mamie Van Doren, and Alan Freed's *Go,
Johnny, Go!* (1959), which also featured two other
singers who had tragically short lives, Ritchie
Valens (1941–1959) and Jackie Wilson (1934–
1984). Vincent had a role in *Hot Rod Gang* (1958;
Fury Unleashed), for which the ads promised 'Crazy
kids living to a wild rock and roll beat!'. He also
had cameo roles in two early '60s British pop
movies, *It's Trad Dad* (1962; *Ring-A-Ding Rhythm*)
and *Live It Up* (1963; *Sing and Swing*). Vincent
died in 1971 from a perforated ulcer.

DEL SHANNON
1939 ★ 1990
AND
ROY ORBISON
1936 ★ 1988

Finally Del Shannon and Roy Orbison can also be
found in the nether world of the pop film. Shannon,
like Vincent, was in *It's Trad Dad*, and also
Daytona Beach Weekend (1965). However, Orbison
has the privilege of starring in the oddest of these
movies, *The Fastest Guitar Alive* (1966), playing a
spy in the American Civil War who has a shotgun
hidden in his guitar.

'LET'S HEAD THEM OFF AT THE PASS' – THE COWBOY STARS

The western was the mainstay of the B-movie for nearly 30 years, until the genre was adopted by television, where 'Gunsmoke', 'The Virginian' et al proved immensely popular. But, until the late '50s, Roy Rogers, Gene Autry, Audie Murphy and the like were big-screen heroes to a million and one schoolkids, nowadays constant fodder for nostalgia pieces on Hollywood's vanished B-movies and Saturday morning serials.

WILD BILL ELLIOTT
1903 ★ 1965

'Wild Bill' Elliott typifies this brand of western hero, starring in a never-ending stream of routine movies and cliffhangers, with titles like *Overland with Kit Carson* (1939), *Vengeance of the West* (1942) and *Sheriff of Redwood Valley* (1946). The ex-rodeo rider had started his acting career playing bit roles, often in A-productions like *Gold Diggers of 1933* (1933) and *Wonder Bar* (1934), under the name Gordon Elliott. His break came when Columbia starred him in the 15-episode serial *The Great Adventures of Wild Bill Hickock* (1938), in which he played a marshal who comes up against the Phantom Raiders, a group of cattle rustlers. Not exactly an original story, but it proved popular,

provided Elliott with his distinctive nickname and launched him on a career as a cowboy star. Two years later he was among the top ten western stars, a position he was to maintain until the mid-1950s. By the late '50s, with the B-western slowly disappearing, Elliott starred in a handful of routine detective films. His final movie was *Footsteps in the Night* (1957). Elliott then turned to work as a spokesman for Viceroy cigarettes and television host for his old movies, before he died of cancer on 26 November 1965.

SMILEY BURNETTE
1911 ★ 1967

Smiley Burnette is the archetypal B-movie western sidekick. He was frequently seen as the comic relief in Roy Rogers, Gene Autry and Charles Starrett westerns and enlivened many a routine oater until his early retirement in 1953. Burnette later found further fame on television, in the series 'Petticoat Junction' (1963–69), which also provided constant employment for another western character actor, Edgar Buchanan. Smiley Burnette's involvement with the series was cut short by his death from leukemia in 1967.

BELOW RIGHT
Smiley Burnette (left) with Sunset Carson (centre) in *Bordertown Trail* (1944).

BELOW LEFT
Wild Bill Elliott, who won first place in a rodeo competition at the age of 16, went on to become one of the top ten western stars throughout the 1940s and early '50s.
■ ■ ■

AUDIE MURPHY
1924 ★ 1971

Perhaps the greatest western B-movie star, with the exception of John Wayne who went on to far greater things, was Audie Murphy. He had already earned quite a reputation prior to his film career as America's most decorated soldier of World War II. Murphy had tried to enlist in the Marines and paratroops, both of whom turned him down as underweight. After leaving the army he appeared on the 5 July 1945 cover of *Life* magazine, which prompted James Cagney to invite him to Hollywood. He made his debut in *Beyond Glory* (1948), and struggled for a while to make his mark. However, by the '50s he was an established cowboy star. He appeared in John Huston's notorious *The Red Badge of Courage* (1951), which MGM butchered into a short running time of 69 minutes before its release. Murphy supposedly had problems playing a coward in this American Civil War movie. Presumably he had fewer problems starring in a cinema version of his autobiography, *To Hell and Back* (1955).

Throughout the '50s Murphy was able to alternate starring parts in programmers with roles in A-movies, such as *The Quiet American* (1957)

based on the novel by Graham Greene and a second Huston movie, *The Unforgiven* (1960). But his best film of this period was *Night Passage* (1957), a fine western in which he supported James Stewart. After this the movies were, in most part, tired rehashes of his past successes. He died on 28 May 1971 in a plane crash outside Atlanta, Georgia.

TIM HOLT
1918 ★ 1973

Murphy was undoubtedly a bigger star than Tim Holt, son of western star Jack Holt, but his best films could not match the three classics in which Holt appeared: Orson Welles' *The Magnificent Ambersons* (1942), as the family's spoilt son; a supporting role as Virgil Earp in John Ford's magnificent western *My Darling Clementine* (1946); and as one of three gold prospectors in John Huston's *The Treasure of the Sierra Madre* (1948). But otherwise it was strictly routine westerns for Holt, although he can also be seen as a cavalryman in *Stagecoach* (1939). By 1957 he was trying his hand at science fiction in *The Monster That Challenged the World* (1957). By 1971 his stock had fallen so low that he was appearing in Herschell Gordon Lewis's grade Z *This Stuff'll Kill Ya!* (1971). However, by this time Holt was concentrating entirely on his work in radio, where he was employed when he died from brain cancer in 1973.

STAGECOACH HOLD-UP SETS STAGE FOR MURDER!

TIM HOLT in STAGECOACH KID
with RICHARD MARTIN · THURSTON HALL
JEFF DONNELL · JOE SAWYER

was perfectly paired with Edmund Gwenn as Kris
Kringle, who goes on trial to prove he is in fact
Santa Claus.

A number of child roles followed, but it was not
until she was cast as the young female lead in *Rebel
without a Cause* (1955) that Wood successfully
made the transition to teen roles. It was enough to
ensure that she was nominated one of the ten Stars
of Tomorrow in 1956, as well as being voted one of
the three Most Promising Female Newcomers of
1956 in the annual Golden Globe Awards. Not bad
for someone who had made her debut only 13 years
earlier! The part in *Rebel* was quickly followed by a
central role in John Ford's classic western *The
Searchers* (1956), in which John Wayne and Jeffrey
Hunter track down the Wood character, who has
been kidnapped and adopted by Indians.

Work was plentiful for the remainder of the '50s,
with starring roles in such big budget productions
as *Kings Go Forth* (1958) alongside Frank Sinatra
and Tony Curtis. She also married film star Robert
Wagner in 1957, which must have been a studio
publicist's delight, attracting much attention from
the fan magazines. They wanted to do a movie
together, but sensibly turned down a number of
comedies about newly weds. Instead they made *All
the Fine Young Cannibals* (1960) together, a routine
melodrama, and harboured unrealized hopes of
filming a third version of Austin Strong's play
'Seventh Heaven'. They were divorced in 1963.

The '60s were to prove her greatest period, but
she first had to go on an 18-month strike for better
roles. This was common practice for many stars who
were tied to a studio contract and dissatisfied with
either the parts or films they were offered. She was
finally rewarded when Elia Kazan requested her for
Splendor in the Grass (1961), an excellent
melodrama about a small-town love affair between
Wood and her co-star Warren Beatty, who was
making his film debut. It certainly ranks amongst
her best films and earned her an Oscar nomination.

■ ■ ■
LEFT
Natalie Wood gives an
excellent performance in
Elia Kazan's *Splendor in
the Grass* (1961), co-
starring with Warren
Beatty.
■ ■ ■
BELOW
Wood as Maria in the
musical *West Side Story*
(1961). Her singing was
dubbed by Marni Nixon,
a service Nixon also
performed for Deborah
Kerr in *The King and I*
and Audrey Hepburn in
My Fair Lady.
■ ■ ■

In the same year she made the popular musical *West Side Story* (1961). However, she was no singer and her songs were dubbed by Marni Nixon. The same happened the next year when she was cast in another musical, as the famous striptease artist Gypsy Rose Lee in *Gypsy* (1962). As the decade progressed she continued to attract good roles. *Love with the Proper Stranger* (1964) opposite Steve McQueen, the overlong but enjoyable comedy *The Great Race* (1965), a version of Tennessee Williams' *This Property is Condemned* (1966) with Robert Redford, which the playwright disliked, and the hit partner-swapping comedy *Bob and Carol and Ted and Alice* (1969).

The remainder of her career was almost exclusively devoted to TV movies and mini-series, 'From Here to Eternity' (1979) being one of the better known. She also remarried Robert Wagner in 1972, following an unsuccessful second marriage to film producer Richard Gregson. They made a second film together, *The Affair* (1973), which was produced for television. Wood finally returned to the big screen in the awful comedy *The Last Married Couple in America* (1979), a tired rehash of *Bob and Carol and Ted and Alice*. The disaster

movie *Meteor* (1980) was even worse, although at least it made use of Wood's command of Russian. Her last film was to be the science fiction movie *Brainstorm* (1983). Her death halted the film's production. On 29 November 1980 she drowned in a lagoon off Santa Catalina island, having apparently slipped when she was drunk, trying to board a dinghy from Wagner's yacht. She was only 43.

'It wasn't a dream palace, of course, it was hard work and all very barnlike. I was a utility actress, I wasn't a 'child star' in the sense of, say, Shirley Temple. But I can sympathize with some of the problems that people like Judy Garland and Jackie Cooper went through. By the time I arrived, there were laws to protect you, to ensure that you got proper schooling and that you actually got to see the money you earned. One particularly difficult time was when I was making The Ghost and Mrs Muir *(1947) and* Miracle on 34th Street *simultaneously. One was a period film, the other a contemporary; in one I was a sweet kid, in the other a bratty kid. That is difficult for a nine-year-old to handle. That's one of the reasons I later went into analysis – to sort all that out.' – Natalie Wood interviewed by David Castell in* Films Illustrated, *July 1980.*

ACTION! – THE PEOPLE BEHIND THE SCENES

The people behind the scenes – the directors, producers, and scriptwriters – are subject to similar pressures and temptations experienced by the more familiar stars. Not surprisingly, there are also a large number of Hollywood casualties amongst the backroom staff.

IRVING THALBERG
1899 ★ 1936

Brooklyn-born Irving Thalberg was the boy-wonder producer of Hollywood during the '20s. He was Head of Production at Universal at only 21 and then, even more successfully, occupied the same position at MGM, where he was responsible for *The Big Parade* (1925) and *Ben Hur* (1926) among many others. Thalberg strove for quality, believing it the secret to greater profit; it certainly worked in his case. During the '30s he produced screen versions of literary classics, such as *Romeo and Juliet* (1936) starring his wife Norma Shearer, Clark Gable's *The Mutiny on the Bounty* (1935) and the all-star *Grand Hotel* (1932). He also signed The Marx Brothers after their rejection by Paramount and the commercial failure of the now classic *Duck Soup* (1933). The Marx Brothers immediately scored two big successes at MGM, with *A Night at the Opera* (1935) and *A Day at the Races* (1937). But he always refused any screen credit, believing 'credit you give yourself isn't worth having'. His untimely death from pneumonia came in September 1936, having suffered from a rheumatic heart condition throughout his life.

ERNST LUBITSCH
1892 ★ 1947

Equally successful as Thalberg was Ernst Lubitsch, the German director who made a series of critically lauded sex comedies, first in Europe and then in Hollywood, for the most part working at Paramount. The 'Lubitsch touch' – a light, charming approach, often using the sexual *double entendre*, frequently set among the rich and above all very cinematic – was legendary, as are his films. They were

sometimes advertised with the slogan, 'It's the Lubitsch touch that means so much'. He was one of the few directors whose name meant something to most cinemagoers. During the early sound period there were the films with Maurice Chevalier, often coupled with Jeanette MacDonald, starting with *The Love Parade* (1929) and lasting until *Trouble in Paradise* (1932), and also taking in the classic *One Hour with You* (1932). The remainder of the '30s included the undervalued *ménage-à-trois* comedy *Design for Living* (1933), two Marlene Dietrich films, *Desire* (1936) and *Angel* (1937), and Greta Garbo's famous *Ninotchka* (1939). Lubitsch died following his sixth heart attack while working on *That Lady in Ermine* (1948).

MICHAEL TODD
1907 ★ 1958

In the '50s there was no bigger showman than Michael Todd. He was famous for his Broadway spectaculars, his marriage to Elizabeth Taylor and for producing the epic *Around the World in 80 Days* (1956). Everything about the film was big: it lasted 178 minutes, featured 44 stars in cameo roles, including Sinatra and Dietrich, was shot in the widescreen Todd-AO process and won the Oscar for the Best Picture of 1956. It was not, however, a great film – it now seems very slow – but it was a great spectacle. He never had the opportunity to improve as a film-maker, for two years later Mike Todd was killed when his plane crashed. He had named it *The Lucky Liz* after his wife.

SAM PECKINPAH
1925 ★ 1984

Many critics considered Sam Peckinpah past his prime by the time of his death, but his last film, *The Osterman Weekend* (1983), belies this theory. Peckinpah made his name with the western, starting with two quiet movies, *The Deadly Companions* (1961) and *Ride the High Country* (1962; *Guns in the Afternoon*), but really rose to

fame with the violent *The Wild Bunch* (1969). This featured his trademark bloodbaths, often shot in slow motion, giving the violence an hypnotic beauty. His films in this vein gained him much notoriety, not least *Straw Dogs* (1971), which caused problems for censors the world over. Each of his films seems to have attracted a cult. There are the quieter films *The Ballad of Cable Hogue* (1970) and *Junior Bonner* (1972), the ultra-violent *Bring Me the Head of Alfredo Garcia* (1974) and, perhaps his best, the beautiful, elegiac western, *Pat Garrett and Billy the Kid* (1973). Most of his films dealt with the effects of violence or the passing of an era, or sometimes both. His original style and unique talent are greatly missed.

RICHARD MARQUAND
1937 ★ 1987

Richard Marquand may have had a promising career ahead of him when he died in 1987. He had directed three critically praised, big budget movies in the '80s. First came the partially successful spy thriller with Donald Sutherland, *Eye of the Needle* (1981), followed by the third part of the Star Wars trilogy, *Return of the Jedi* (1983). But he really

リチャード・マーカンド

made his mark with the gripping thriller *Jagged Edge* (1985), an excellent courtroom mystery starring Jeff Bridges and Glenn Close. However, he also had more than his fair share of clinkers. The dreadful horror movie *The Legacy* (1978) and the awful *Birth of the Beatles* (1979) early on in his career, while his last film was the universally panned *Hearts of Fire* (1987), a rock drama featuring Rupert Everett and Bob Dylan. Despite the handful of good movies and some promise, it is doubtful that Marquand would ever have reached the stature of Peckinpah.

JIM HENSON
1936 ★ 1990

Finally, into the '90s and the sad death of puppeteer Jim Henson, the man behind the successful television series 'Sesame Street' and 'The Muppets' with Frank Oz. Henson also had some success, and a few interesting failures, with the cinema, first with *The Muppet Movie* (1979). A couple more Muppet features followed, but Henson surpassed these with his subsequent movies. First came the all-puppet film *The Dark Crystal* (1982), followed by *Dreamchild* (1985), the story of the girl who provided the original inspiration for Lewis Carroll's Alice from a script by Dennis Potter. His next film unfortunately gained far more publicity, the intermittently interesting *Labyrinth* (1986). His last film, Nic Roeg's *The Witches* (1990), was hardly more successful. But even his failures were of interest. Henson's creations were certainly a success, at least commercially. One year before his death from a massive bacterial infection the Disney organization paid $150 million for the rights to The Muppets.

■ ■ ■
LEFT
Richard Marquand promoting *Return of the Jedi* (1983), the third entry in the Star Wars trilogy.
■ ■ ■
BELOW
Gary Kurtz (left), Jim Henson (centre) and Frank Oz (right) on the set of *The Dark Crystal* (1982).
■ ■ ■

1925 ★ 1985

ROCK HUDSON

Rock Hudson was one of the last major film stars produced by the Hollywood studio system. The studio system schooled young actors and actresses by providing them with training in acting, singing, diction, fencing – in fact any skills that they felt might prove useful. In return for this treatment the studio could use him in as many movies as it wished for a salary, in Hudson's case, of $125 per week. Hudson made good use of this training. He might not have been a great actor, although he was certainly not bad, but he was a great film star.

His first break came when he was signed up by talent agent Henry Wilson, who changed his name

from Roy Scherer to Rock Hudson and introduced him to action director Raoul Walsh. Hudson made his debut in Walsh's *Fighter Squadron* (1948) and the director signed him to a personal contract, which he then sold to Universal, where Hudson could gain more experience. He undoubtedly needed it, reputedly requiring over 30 takes to deliver his one line of dialogue in his debut feature. At Universal he played many parts of varying sizes and during the early '50s gradually moved up the ladder to leading-man status. He appeared in some good westerns and starred in his first film for director Douglas Sirk, the fresh musical comedy *Has Anybody Seen My Gal?* (1952). It was Sirk who directed him in his breakthrough movie, the classic weepie *Magnificent Obsession* (1954). He played a playboy, who is responsible for a woman's (Jane Wyman) blindness and the death of her husband, a leading surgeon. He attempts to right his mistake, becomes a surgeon himself and cures Wyman. Pure melodrama, for which Hudson proved a fine romantic lead.

It was the first in a series of classic melodramas he was to make with Sirk and producer Ross Hunter throughout the '50s. The following year Hudson was reunited with Wyman for the team's best collaboration, *All That Heaven Allows* (1955), a tale of an older woman falling for a younger man and an excellent critique of small-town American life. In fact all the films have a strong undercurrent of social criticism, giving them a power and complexity that their contemporaries lack. This is equally true of the team's third and perhaps best-known movie together, *Written on the Wind* (1956), the story of a rich oil family gradually disintegrating. Hudson's final appearance for Sirk

and Hunter was in *The Tarnished Angels* (1957). He was now established among the world's top five film stars, a position he maintained for a decade.

In between he had been chosen by George Stevens to star in *Giant* (1956), an overblown, ponderous epic, also about the riches brought by oil. It lacked the intensity of Sirk's movies but, typically of Hollywood, it was Stevens' self-important movie which gained all the attention on

release. It brought Hudson his only Oscar nomination and, it must be said, was the actor's favourite of his own films.

In the late '50s Rock Hudson's career changed direction when he was teamed with Doris Day in *Pillow Talk* (1959). The two became a hugely popular team, although they only made three movies together. However, Hudson did appear in a string of similar, sophisticated sex (or what passed for sex in Hollywood during the early '60s) comedies, opposite such glamorous leading ladies as Gina Lollobrigida and Claudia Cardinale. He was well suited to comedy, a talent Sirk had first discovered, perhaps because of his great size and partly from the incongruity of watching such a classically handsome actor involved in slapstick.

But Hudson wanted to stretch himself. In 1966 he left the security of Universal and immediately won his best acting role in John Frankenheimer's excellent paranoia thriller *Seconds* (1966). However, he never really had the acting talent of, for example, Dirk Bogarde, who had found himself in a similar situation in the early '60s. Further

■ ■ ■
LEFT
Rock Hudson and John Wayne may have been past their prime when they made *The Undefeated* (1969), but they were still major stars.
■ ■ ■

■ ■ ■
LEFT
This publicity shot of Rock Hudson, his new wife Phyllis Gates, and their two dogs, was trying to depict the Hudsons as a typical married couple enjoying ordinary domesticity.
■ ■ ■

ABOVE
All That Heaven Allows
(1955), a powerful
melodrama directed by
Douglas Sirk, was Rock
Hudson's second film
with co-star Jane
Wyman.

two-hander with Carol Burnett, and *Camelot*. He did make the occasional movie, of which *Avalanche* (1978) must have been the low point of his career, with its poor continuity, incredible plotting, awful acting and cheapskate special effects.

When he appeared in nine episodes of 'Dynasty' in 1984, Hudson was looking considerably thinner and quite ill. His death from AIDS on 2 October 1985 made his homosexuality, which had been common knowledge in Hollywood, front page news. News of his homosexuality had nearly broken in the '50s, when the scandal magazine *Confidential* got hold of the story. However, Hudson was too big a star for Universal to lose and so they sacrificed another of their contract actors, Rory Calhoun. They gave 'Confidential' the story of Calhoun's early prison record and were able to cover up the Rock Hudson story.

The public news of Hudson's homosexuality has added a melancholy aspect to his career, particularly the fan magazine stories about Hollywood's most eligible bachelor. Perhaps even sadder was his short-lived, studio-arranged marriage to Phyllis Gates, his agent's secretary. But the real tragedy was that Rock Hudson could not be accepted for what he was, a first-rate film star and a fine comic actor, who also happened to be homosexual.

serious roles did not come Hudson's way.

As the good roles in mainstream Hollywood comedies and action movies dried up for Hudson in the late '60s, he turned to television with amazing success. His television series, the cop show 'McMillan and Wife' (1971–76), was exceptionally popular. The format was very similar to that of the old Hollywood movies: a rich, wisecracking, happily married couple solving a series of crimes. During this period Hudson also had some success on the stage, starring in the musicals *I Do, I Do,* a

Rock Hudson in the '50s fan magazines:
'Why should I date some glamour girl, just for publicity?'

'I can't imagine why the public doesn't get bored with me as a person anyway. I have no phobias, quirks or neuroses . . . I'm strictly the unsensational type.'

'Phyllis is going to be plain Mrs Housewife. I'm going to mow the lawn on Saturdays. And we hope to raise a large family. That's the way to make a marriage work in Hollywood.'

OTHER STARS 1980–1989

Gloria Grahame (1925–1981)

Gloria Grahame was an excellent actress who deserved better movies than she received, as lasting success just seemed to allude her. Nevertheless, her career has many memorable moments. Grahame first made an impact in a small role as a small-town flirt and prostitute in Frank Capra's classic It's a Wonderful Life *(1946), which she followed with an Oscar-nominated supporting performance in the thriller* Crossfire *(1947). The '50s were her greatest period, beginning with a superb study of violence,* In a Lonely Place *(1950), opposite Humphrey Bogart. She won an Oscar as Best Supporting Actress for her performance in* The Bad and the Beautiful *(1952), had boiling coffee thrown in her face in* The Big Heat *(1953), a surprisingly vicious scene for the period, and had a leading role in the hit musical* Oklahoma! *(1955). As the decade drew to a close the roles dried up, although Grahame still appeared in the occasional movie up until her death from cancer in 1981.*

John Belushi (1949–1982)

John Belushi was first noticed on television in NBC's famous comedy programme, 'Saturday Night Live', where he teamed up with Dan Aykroyd to present the characters Jake and Elwood, the Blues Brothers. The show's success led to an equally successful film, the college comedy National Lampoon's Animal House *(1978). Belushi followed this with Steven Spielberg's* 1941 *(1979) and his most enduring film, the cult hit* The Blues Brothers *(1980), also starring Aykroyd. However, the remainder of his films were, at best, forgettable. Belushi died on 5 March 1982 from acute cocaine and heroin intoxication, aged only 33.*

BELOW LEFT
Gloria Grahame with Glenn Ford in the Fritz Lang thriller *The Big Heat* (1953).

BELOW RIGHT
The publicity poster for the cult-hit *The Blues Brothers* (1980) starring John Belushi and Dan Aykroyd as Jake and Elwood Blues.

Warren Oates (1928–1982)

Warren Oates is one of the great cult actors of the '70s, appearing in films directed by Monte Hellman, Peter Fonda, Terence Malik and, of course, the great Sam Peckinpah. Oates' slightly seedy appearance, equally suited to the perpetual loser or the vicious

thug, was always welcome. He starred in the bloody western The Wild Bunch *(1969), the cult road movie* Two Lane Blacktop *(1971) and the violent* Bring Me the Head of Alfredo Garcia *(1974). But one of his best performances is frequently overlooked; the title role in John Milius' gangster flick* Dillinger *(1973). He died at his home on 3 April 1982.*

Carolyn Jones (1933–1983)

Carolyn Jones will be forever identified as Morticia from the black comedy television series 'The Addams Family' (1964–65). However, at one time she seemed to have a highly promising cinema career ahead of her. Jones appeared in the '50s cult classics The Big Heat *(1953),* House of Wax *(1953),*

Invasion of the Body Snatchers (1956), and Baby Face Nelson *(1957). This was followed by an Oscar nomination for her performance in* Bachelor Party *(1957), the female lead in a good Kirk Douglas western,* The Last Train from Gun Hill *(1959), and a role in a Frank Capra movie,* A Hole in the Head *(1959). Unfortunately, her career never took off as expected. She died from cancer on 3 August 1983.*

Andy Warhol (1928–1987)

Andy Warhol was the most famous of America's underground film-makers of the '60s. His early films were simple shorts with self-explanatory titles such as Kiss *(1963),* Blow Job *(1964) and* Sleep *(1964). His ambition increased with* Chelsea Girls *(1966), a three and a half hour epic shown entirely on split screen. Warhol was even more famous away from the screen, for his art, for the celebrities at the Factory and for his involvement with The Velvet Underground. He later lent his name to films directed by others, mostly Paul Morrissey, including* Trash *(1970) and the 3-D* Flesh for Frankenstein *(1973; Andy Warhol's Frankenstein). He died in 1987 while recovering from a gall bladder operation.*

Divine (1945–1988)

Divine won lasting fame in the trash cult movies of John Waters, including starring roles in Pink Flamingos *(1972),* Female Trouble *(1974), Polyester *(1981) and* Hairspray *(1988). Away from the Waters stable, Divine turned his hand to stage, with* Women Behind Bars, *and music, with the hit 'You Think You're a Man'. Divine was the 'creation' of Glenn Milstead, who was enjoying further success in straight roles at the time of his death.*

Jill Ireland (1936–1990)

British actress Jill Ireland appeared in numerous British movies of the '50s and early '60s, such as Three Men in a Boat *(1956),* Carry on Nurse *(1959) and* Hell Drivers *(1957). The latter also starred her husband David McCallum. When McCallum went to Hollywood to appear in the television series 'The Man from U.N.C.L.E.' (1964–67), Ireland went with him and occasionally appeared as a guest star on the show. Their relationship did not last and after her divorce in 1967 she married Charles Bronson. Ireland appeared in most of his films throughout the '70s, including* Valdez is Coming *(1970),* The Mechanic *(1972),* The Valachi Papers *(1972),* Breakheart Pass *(1975), and* Love and Bullets *(1978). She published a book,* Life Wish, *in 1986 about her fight against cancer, from which she died in 1990.*

■ ■ ■

LEFT
Artist and underground film-maker Andy Warhol directing *Chelsea Girls* (1966).

■ ■ ■

BELOW LEFT
Divine's name is synonymous with trash movie director John Waters, who gave Divine (left) starring roles in many of his films, including *Female Trouble* (1974).

■ ■ ■

BELOW
Jill Ireland in *Valdez is Coming* (1970); she co-starred with her second husband Charles Bronson repeatedly during the '70s.

■ ■ ■

INDEX